HOW TO ATTRACT MONEY

Maple Spring Publishing Titles

PRINT, EPUB & AUDIO

Crystallizing Public Opinion

Think and Grow Rich

The Richest Man in Babylon

The Power of Your Subconscious Mind

The Magic of Believing

The Science of Getting Rich

The Prince

Letters from a Stoic

The Mystery of the Blue Train

The Dynamic Laws of Prosperity

The Great Gatsby

How to Attract Money with Bonus

Riches Are Your Right with Bonus

This is It with Bonus

Quiet Moments With God with Bonus

EPUB & AUDIO

The Art of War

The Science of Being Great

Your Invisible Power

At Your Command

The Magic Story

Think and Grow Rich Deluxe Original Edition

T.N.T.: It Rocks the Earth

Believe in Yourself

How to Use the Power of Prayer

This is It

Quiet Moments with God

The Power of Your Subconscious Mind with Bonus

The Greatest thing in the World

ORIGINAL CLASSIC EDITION

HOW TO ATTRACT MONEY

FEATURES BONUS BOOK: BELIEVE IN YOURSELF

JOSEPH MURPHY

Published 2024 by Maple Spring Publishing

Front cover design by David Rheinhardt of Pyrographx

Interior design by Meghan Day Healey of Story Horse, LLC.

Library of Congress Cataloging-in-Publication Data is available upon request

ISBN: 979-8-3505-0055-4

10 9 8 7 6 5 4 3 2 1

Contents

1

Your Right to Be Rich

It is your right to be rich. You are here to lead the abundant life, and be happy, radiant, and free. You should, therefore, have all the money you need to lead a full, happy, prosperous life.

There is no virtue in poverty; the latter is a mental disease, and it should be abolished from the face of the earth. You are here to grow, expand, and unfold, spiritually, mentally, and materially. You have the inalienable right to fully develop and express yourself along all lines. You should surround yourself with beauty and luxury.

Why be satisfied with just enough to go around when you can enjoy the riches of the Infinite? In this book you will learn to make friends with money, and you will always have a surplus. Your desire to be rich is a desire for a fuller, happier, more wonderful life. It is a cosmic urge. It is good and very good.

Begin to see money in its true significance—as a symbol of exchange. It means to you freedom from want, and beauty, luxury, abundance, and refinement.

As you read this chapter, you are probably saying, "I want more money." "I am worthy of a higher salary than I am receiving."

I believe most people are inadequately compensated. One of the causes many people do not have more money is that they are silently or openly condemning it. They refer to money as "filthy lucre," or "Love of money is the root of all evil," etc. Another reason they do not prosper is that they have a sneaky, subconscious feeling there is some virtue in poverty; this subconscious pattern may be due to early childhood training, superstition, or it could be based on a false interpretation of the Scriptures.

There is no virtue in poverty; it is a disease like any other mental disease. If you were physically ill, you would think there was something wrong with you; you would seek help, or do something about the condition at once. Likewise if you do not have money constantly circulating in your life, there is something radically wrong with you.

Money is only a symbol; it has taken many forms as a medium of exchange down through the centuries, such as salt, beads, and trinkets of various kinds. In early times man's wealth was determined by the number of sheep or oxen he had. It is much more convenient to write a check than to carry some sheep around with you to pay your bills.

God does not want you to live in a hovel or go hungry. God *wants* you to be happy, prosperous, and successful. God is always successful in all His undertakings, whether He makes a star or a cosmos!

You may wish to make a trip around the world, study art in foreign countries, go to college, or send your children to a superior school. You certainly wish to bring your children up in lovely surroundings, so that they might learn to appreciate beauty, order, symmetry, and proportion.

You were born to succeed, to win, to conquer all difficulties, and have all your faculties fully developed. If there is financial lack in your life, do something about it.

Get away immediately from all superstitious beliefs about money. Do not ever regard money as evil or filthy. If you do, you cause it to take wings and fly away from you. Remember that you lose what you condemn.

Suppose, for example, you found gold, silver, lead, copper, or iron in the ground. Would you pronounce these things evil? God pronounced all things good. The evil comes from man's darkened understanding, from his unillumined mind, from his false interpretation of life, and his misuse of Divine Power. Uranium, lead, or some other metal could have been used as a medium of exchange. We use paper bills, checks, etc.; surely the piece of paper is not evil; neither is the check. Physicists and scientists know today that the only difference between one metal and another is the number and rate of motion of the electrons revolving around a central nucleus. They are now changing one metal into another through a bombardment of the atoms in the powerful cyclotron. Gold under certain conditions becomes mercury. It will only be a little while until gold, silver, and other metals will be made synthetically in the chemical laboratory. I cannot imagine seeing anything evil in electrons, neutrons, protons, and isotopes.

The piece of paper in your pocket is composed of electrons and protons arranged differently; their number and rate of motion is different; that is the only way the paper differs from the silver in your pocket.

Some people will say, "Oh, people kill for money. They steal for money!" It has been associated with countless crimes, but that does not make it evil.

A man may give another $50 to kill someone; he has misused money in using it for a destructive purpose. You can use electricity to kill someone or light the house. You can use water to quench the baby's thirst, or use it to drown the child. You can use fire to warm the child, or burn it to death.

Another illustration would be if you brought some earth from your garden, put it in your coffee cup for breakfast, that would be your evil; yet the earth is not evil; neither is the coffee. The earth is displaced; it belongs in your garden.

Similarly if a needle were stuck in your thumb, it would be your evil; the needle or pin belongs in the pin cushion, not in your thumb.

We know the forces or the elements of nature are not evil; it depends on our use of them whether they bless or hurt us.

A man said to me one time, "I am broke. I do not like money; it is the root of all evil."

Love of money to the exclusion of everything else will cause you to become lopsided and unbalanced. You are here to use your power or authority wisely. Some men crave power; others crave money. If you set your heart on money, and say, "That is all I want. I am going to give all my attention to amassing money; nothing else matters," you can get money and attain a fortune, but you have forgotten that you are here to lead a balanced life. "Man does not live by bread alone."

For example, if you belong to some cult or religious group, and become fanatical about it, excluding yourself from your friends, society, and social activities, you will become unbalanced, inhibited, and frustrated. Nature insists on a balance. If all your time is devoted to external things and possessions, you will find yourself hungry for peace of mind, harmony, love, joy, or perfect health. You will find you cannot buy anything that is real. You can amass a fortune, or have millions of dollars; this is not evil or bad. Love of money to the exclusion of everything else results in frustration, disappointment, and disillusionment; in that sense it is the root of your evil.

By making money your sole aim, you simply made a wrong choice. You thought that was all you wanted, but you found after all your efforts that it was not only the money you needed. What you really desired was true place, peace of mind, and abundance. You could have the million or many millions, if you wanted them, and still have peace of mind, harmony, perfect health, and Divine expression.

Everyone wants enough money, and not just enough to go around. He wants abundance and to spare; he should have it. The urges, desires, and impulses we have for food, clothing, homes, better means of transportation, expression, procreation, and abundance are all God-given, Divine, and good, but we may misdirect these impulses, desires, and urges resulting in evil or negative experiences in our lives.

Man does not have an evil nature; there is no evil nature in you; it is God, the Universal Wisdom, or Life seeking expression through you.

For example, a boy wants to go to college, but he does not have enough money. He sees other boys in the neighborhood going off to college and the university; his desire increases. He says to himself, "I want an education, too." Such a youth may steal and embezzle money for the purpose of going to college. The desire to go to college was basically and fundamentally good; he misdirected that desire or urge by violating the laws of society, the cosmic law of harmony, or the golden rule; then he finds himself in trouble.

However if this boy knew the laws of mind, and his unqualified capacity through the use of the Spiritual Power to go to college, he would be free and not in jail. Who put him in jail? He placed himself there. The policeman who locked him up in prison was an instrument of the man-made laws which he violated. He first imprisoned himself in his mind by stealing and hurting others. Fear and a guilt consciousness followed; this is the prison of the mind followed by the prison walls made of bricks and stones.

Money is a symbol of God's opulence, beauty, refinement, and abundance, and it should be used wisely, judiciously, and constructively to bless humanity in countless ways. It is merely a symbol of the economic health of the nation. When your blood is circulating freely, you are healthy. When money is circulating freely in your life, you are economically healthy. When people begin to hoard money, to put it away in tin boxes, and become charged with fear, there is economic illness.

The crash of 1929 was a psychological panic; it was fear seizing the minds of people everywhere. It was a sort of negative, hypnotic spell.

You are living in a subjective and objective world. You must not neglect the spiritual food, such as peace of mind, love, beauty, harmony, joy, and laughter.

Knowledge of the spiritual power is the means to the Royal Road to Riches of all kinds, whether your desire is spiritual, mental, or material. The student of the laws of mind, or the student of the spiritual principle, believes and knows absolutely that regardless of the economic situation, stock market fluctuation, depression, strikes, war, other conditions, or circumstances, he will always be amply supplied regardless of what form money may take. The reason for this is he abides in the consciousness of wealth. The student has convinced himself in his mind that wealth is forever flowing freely in his life, and that there is always a Divine surplus. Should there be a war tomorrow, and all the student's present holdings become valueless, as the German marks did after the First World War, he would still attract wealth, and be cared for regardless of the form the new currency took.

Wealth is a state of consciousness; it is a mind conditioned to Divine supply forever flowing. The scientific thinker looks at money or wealth like the tide; i.e., it goes out, but it always comes back. The tides never fail; neither will man's supply when he trusts a tireless, changeless, immortal Presence which is Omnipresent, and flows ceaselessly. The man who knows the workings of the subconscious mind is never, therefore, worried about the economic situation, stock market panics, devaluation, or inflation of currency, since he abides in the consciousness of God's eternal supply. Such a man is always supplied and watched over by an overshadowing Presence. *Behold the fowls of the air: for they sow not, neither do they reap, nor gather into barns; yet your heavenly Father feedeth them. Are ye not much better than they?* MATTHEW 6:26.

As you consciously commune with the Divine-Presence claiming and knowing that It leads and guides you in all your ways, that It is a Lamp unto your feet, and a Light on your path, you will be Divinely prospered and sustained beyond your wildest dreams.

Here is a simple way for you to impress your subconscious mind with the idea of constant supply or wealth: Quiet the wheels of your mind. Relax! Let go! Immobilize the attention. Get into a sleepy, drowsy, meditative state of mind; this reduces effort to the minimum; then in a quiet, relaxed, passive way reflect on the following simple truths: Ask yourself where do ideas come from? Where does wealth come from? Where did you come from? Where did your brain and your mind come from? You will be led back to the One Source.

You find yourself on a spiritual, working basis now. It will no longer insult your intelligence to realize that wealth is a state of mind. Take this little phrase; repeat it slowly four or five minutes three or four times a day quietly to yourself, particularly before you go to sleep: "Money is forever circulating freely in my life, and there is always a Divine surplus." As you do this regularly and systematically, the idea of wealth will be conveyed to your deeper mind, and you will develop a wealth consciousness. Idle, mechanical repetition will not succeed in building the consciousness of wealth. Begin to feel the truth of what you affirm. You know what you are doing, and why you are doing it. You know your deeper self is responsive to what you consciously accept as true.

In the beginning people who are in financial difficulties do not get results with such affirmations as, "I am wealthy," "I am prosperous," "I am successful"; such statements may cause their conditions to get worse. The reason is the subconscious mind will only accept the dominant of two ideas, or the dominant mood or feeling. When they say, "I am prosperous," their feeling of lack is greater, and something within them says, "No, you are not prosperous, you are broke." The feeling of lack is dominant so that each affirmation calls forth the mood of lack, and more lack becomes theirs. The way to overcome this for beginners is to affirm what the conscious and subconscious mind will agree on; then there will be no contradiction. Our subconscious mind accepts our beliefs, feelings, convictions, and what we consciously accept as true.

A man could engage the cooperation of his subconscious mind by saying, "I am prospering every day." "I am growing in wealth and in wisdom every day." "Every day my wealth is multiplying." "I am advancing, growing, and moving forward financially." These and similar statements would not create any conflict in the mind.

For instance if a salesman has only ten cents in his pocket, he could easily agree that he would have more tomorrow. If he sold a pair of shoes tomorrow, there is nothing within him which says his sales could not increase. He could use statements, such as, "My sales are increasing every day." "I am advancing and moving forward." He would find these would be sound psychologically, acceptable to his mind, and produce desirable fruit.

The spiritually advanced student who quietly, knowingly, and feelingly says, "I am prosperous," "I am successful," "I am wealthy," gets wonderful results also. Why would this be true? When they think, feel, or say, "I am prosperous," they mean God is All Supply or Infinite Riches, and what is true of God is true of them. When they say, "I am wealthy," they know God is Infinite Supply, the Inexhaustible, Treasure-House, and what is true of God is, therefore, true of them, for God is within them.

Many men get wonderful results by dwelling on three abstract ideas, such as health, wealth, and success. *Health* is a Divine Reality or quality of God. *Wealth* is of God; it is eternal and endless. *Success* is of God; God is always successful in all His undertakings.

The way they produce remarkable results is to stand before a mirror as they shave, and repeat for five or ten minutes: "Health, wealth, and success." They do not say, "I am healthy," or "I am successful"; they create no opposition in their minds. They are quiet and relaxed; thus the mind is receptive and passive; then they repeat these words. Amazing results follow. All they are doing is identifying with truths that are eternal, changeless, and timeless.

You can develop a wealth consciousness. Put the principles enunciated and elaborated on in this book to practice, and your desert will rejoice and blossom as the rose.

I worked with a young boy in Australia many years ago who wanted to become a physician and surgeon, but he had no money; nor had he graduated from high school. For expenses he used to clean out doctors' offices, wash windows, and do odd repair jobs. He told me that every night as he went to sleep, he used to see a diploma on a wall with his name in big, bold letters. He used to clean and shine the diplomas in the medical building where he worked; it was not hard for him to engrave the diploma in his mind and develop it there. I do not know how long he continued this imaging, but it must have been for some months.

Results followed as he persisted. One of the doctors took a great liking to this young boy, and after training him in the art of sterilizing instruments, giving hypodermic injections, and other miscellaneous first aid work, he became a technical assistant in his office. The doctor sent him to high school and also to college at his expense.

Today this man is a prominent doctor in Montreal, Canada. He had a dream! A clear image in his mind! *His wealth was in his mind.*

Wealth is your idea, desire, talent, urge for service, capacity to give to mankind, your ability for usefulness to society, and your love for humanity in general.

This young boy operated a great law unconsciously. Troward says, "Having seen the end, you have willed the means to the realization of the end." The *end* in this boy's case was to be a physician. To imagine, see, and feel the reality of being a doctor now, to live with that idea, sustain it, nourish it, and to love it until through his imagination it penetrated the layers of the subconscious, becoming a conviction, paved the way to the fulfillment of his dreams.

He could have said, "I have no education." "I do not know the right people." "I am too old to go to school now." "I have no money; it would take years, and I am not intelligent." He would then be beaten before he started. His wealth was in his use of the Spiritual Power within him which responded to his thought.

The means or the way in which our prayer is answered is always hidden from us except that occasionally we may intuitively perceive a part of the process. *My ways are past finding out.* The *ways* are not known. The only thing man has to do is to imagine and accept the end in his mind, and leave its unfoldment to the subjective wisdom within.

Oftentimes the question is asked, "What should I do after meditating on the end and accepting my desire in consciousness?" The answer is simple: You will be compelled to do whatever is necessary for the unfoldment of your ideal. The law of the subconscious is compulsion. The law of life is action and reaction. What we do is the automatic response to our inner movements of the mind, inner feeling, and conviction.

A few months ago as I went to sleep, I imagined I was reading one of my most popular books, *Magic of Faith* in French. I began to realize and imagine this book going into all French-speaking nations. For several weeks I did this every night, falling asleep with the imaginary French edition of *Magic of Faith* in my hands.

Just before Christmas in 1954, I received a letter from a leading publisher in Paris, France, enclosing a contract drawn up, asking me to sign it, giving him permission to publish and promote abroad to all French-speaking countries the French edition of *Magic of Faith.*

You might ask me what did I do about the publishing of this book after prayer? I would have to say, "Nothing!" The subjective wisdom took over, and brought it to pass in its own way, which was a far better way than any method I could consciously desire.

All of our external movements, motions, and actions follow the inner movements of the mind. Inner action precedes all outer action. Whatever steps you take physically, or what you seem to do objectively, will all be a part of a pattern which you were compelled to fulfill.

Accepting the end wills the means to the realization of the end. Believe that you have it now, and you shall receive it.

We must cease denying our good. Realize that the only thing that keeps us from the riches that lie all around us is our mental attitude, or the way we look at God, life, and the world in general. Know, believe, and act on the positive assumption that there is no reason why you cannot have, be, and do whatever you wish to accomplish through the great laws of God.

Your knowledge of how your mind works is your saviour and redeemer. Thought and feeling are your destiny. You possess everything by right of consciousness. The consciousness of health produces health; the consciousness of wealth produces wealth. The world seems to deny or oppose what you pray for; your senses sometimes mock and laugh at you.

If you say to your friend, you are opening up a new business for yourself, he may proceed to give you all the reasons why you are bound to fail. If you are susceptible to his hypnotic spell, he may instill fear of failure in your mind. As you become aware of the spiritual power which is one and indivisible, and responds to your thought, you will reject the darkness and ignorance of the world, and know that you possess all the equipment, power, and knowledge to succeed.

To walk on the Royal Road to Riches, you must not place obstacles and impediments on the pathway of others; neither must you be jealous or envious of others. Actually when you entertain these negative states of mind, you are hurting and injuring yourself, because you are thinking and feeling it. "The suggestion," as Quimby said, "you give to another, you are giving to yourself." This is the reason that the law of the golden rule is a cosmic, divine law.

I am sure you have heard men say, "That fellow has a racket." "He is a racketeer." "He is getting money dishonestly." "He is a faker." "I knew him when he had nothing." "He is crooked, a thief, and a swindler." If you analyze the man who talks like that, he is usually in want or suffering from some financial or physical illness. Perhaps his former, college friends went up the ladder of success and excelled him; now he is bitter and envious of their progress. In many instances this is the cause of his downfall. Thinking negatively of these classmates, and condemning their wealth, causes the wealth and prosperity he is praying for to vanish and flee away. He is condemning the things he is praying for. He is praying two ways. On the one hand he is saying, "God is prospering me," and in the next breath, silently or audibly, he is saying, "I resent that fellow's wealth." Always make it a special point to bless the other person, and rejoice in his prosperity and success; when you do, you bless and prosper yourself.

If you go into the bank, and you see your competitor across the street deposit twenty times more than you do, or you see him deposit ten thousand dollars, rejoice and be exceedingly glad to see God's abundance being manifested through one of his sons. You are then blessing and exalting what you are praying for. What you bless, you multiply. What you condemn, you lose.

If you are working in a large organization, and you are silently thinking and resenting the fact you are underpaid, that you are not appreciated, and that you deserve more money and greater recognition, you are subconsciously severing your ties with that organization. You are setting a law in motion; then the superintendent or manager says to you, "We have to let you go." You dismissed yourself. The manager was simply the instrument through which your own negative, mental state was confirmed. In other words he was a messenger telling you what you conceived as true about yourself. It was an example of the law of action and reaction. The action was the internal movement of your mind; the *reaction* was the response of the outer world to conform to your inner thinking.

Perhaps as you read this, you are thinking of someone who has prospered financially by taking advantage of others, by defrauding them, in selling them unsound investments in property, etc. The answer to this is obvious, because if we rob, cheat, or defraud another, we do the same to ourselves. In reality in this case we are actually hurting or robbing from ourselves. We are in a mood of lack in the first place, which is bound to attract loss to us. The loss may come in many ways; it may come in loss of health, prestige, peace of mind, social status, sickness in the home, or in business. It may not necessarily come in loss of money. We must not be shortsighted and think that the loss has to come just in dollars and cents.

Isn't it a wonderful feeling to place your head on the pillow at night, and feel you are at peace with the whole world, and that your heart is full of goodwill toward all? There are some people who have accumulated money the wrong way, as by tramping on others, trickery, deceit, and chicanery. What is the price? Sometimes it is mental and physical disease, guilt complexes, insomnia, or hidden fears. As one man said to me, "Yes, I rode roughshod over others. I got what I wanted, but I got cancer doing it." He realized he had attained his wealth in the wrong way.

You can be wealthy and prosperous without hurting anyone. Many men are constantly robbing themselves; they steal from themselves: peace of mind, health, joy, inspiration, happiness, and the laughter of God. They may say that they have never stolen, but is it true? Every time we resent another, or are jealous, or envious of another's wealth or success, we are stealing from ourselves. These are the thieves and robbers which Jesus cast out of the temple; likewise you must cast them out incisively and decisively. Do not let them live in your mind. Cut their heads off with the fire of right thought and feeling.

I remember in the early days of the war reading about a woman in Brooklyn, New York, who went around from store to store buying up all the coffee she could. She knew it was going to be rationed; she was full of fear that there would not be enough for her. She bought as much as she could, and stored it in the cellar. That evening she went to church services. When she came home, burglars had broken down the door, stolen not only the coffee, but silverware, money, jewelry, and other things.

This good woman said what they all say: "Why did this happen to me when I was at church? I never stole from anyone."

Is this true? Was she not in the consciousness of lack and fear when she began to hoard supplies of coffee? Her mood and fear of lack was sufficient to bring about loss in her home and possessions. She did not have to put her hand on the cash register or rob a bank; her fear of lack produced lack. This is the reason that many people who are what society calls "good citizens" suffer loss. They are good in the worldly sense; i.e., they pay their taxes; they obey the laws, vote regularly, and are generous to charities, but they are resentful of others' possessions, their wealth, or social position. If they would like to take money when no one was looking, such an attitude is definitely and positively a state of lack, and may cause the person who indulges in such a mental state to attract charlatans or knaves who may swindle or cheat them in some business transaction.

Before the outer thief robs us, we have first robbed ourselves. There must be an inner thief, before the outer one appears.

A man can have a guilt complex, and be accusing himself constantly. I knew such a man; he was very honest as a teller in a bank. He never stole any money, but he had an illicit romance; he was supporting another woman, and denying his family. He lived in fear that he would be discovered; a deep sense of guilt resulted. Fear follows guilt. Fear causes a contraction of the muscles and mucous membranes; acute sinusitis developed. Medication only gave him temporary relief.

I explained to this client the cause of his trouble, and told him the cure was to give up his outside affair. He said he couldn't; she was his soul mate, and that he had tried. He was always condemning and accusing himself.

One day he was accused by one of the officials of the bank of having embezzled some money; it looked serious for him, as the evidence was circumstantial. He became panic stricken, and realized that the only reason he was wrongfully accused was that he had been accusing and condemning himself. He saw how mind operates. Inasmuch as he was always accusing himself on the inner plane, he would be accused on the outer.

He broke off the relationship immediately with the other woman due to the shock of being accused of embezzling, and began to pray for Divine harmony and understanding between himself and the bank official. He began to claim, "There is nothing hidden that is not revealed. The peace of God reigns supreme in the minds and hearts of all concerned."

Truth prevailed. The whole matter was dissolved in the light of truth. Another young man was discovered as the culprit. The bank teller knew that only through prayer was he saved from a jail sentence.

The great law is, "As you would that men should think about you, think you about them in the same manner. As you would that men should feel about you, feel you also about them in like manner."

Say from your heart, "I wish for every man who walks the earth, what I wish for myself. The sincere wish of my heart is, therefore, peace, love, joy, abundance, and God's blessings to all men everywhere." Rejoice and be glad in the progression, advancement, and prosperity of all men. Whatever you claim as true for yourself, claim it for all men everywhere. If you pray for happiness and peace of mind, let your claim be peace and happiness for all. Do not ever try and deprive another of any joy. If you do, you deprive yourself. When the ship comes in for your friend, it comes in for you also.

If someone is promoted in your organization, be glad and happy. Congratulate him, rejoice in his advancement and recognition. If you are angry or resentful, you are demoting yourself. Do not try and withhold from another his God-given birthright to happiness, success, achievement, abundance, and all good things.

Jesus said, "Sow up for yourselves treasures in heaven, where the moth and the rust doth not consume, and where thieves cannot break through and steal." Hatred and resentment rot and corrode the heart causing us to become full of scars, impurities, toxins, and poisons.

The treasures of heaven are the truths of God which we possess in our soul. Fill your minds with peace, harmony, faith, joy, honesty, integrity, loving kindness, and gentleness; then you will be sowing for yourself treasures in the heavens of your own mind.

If you are seeking wisdom regarding investments, or if you are worried about your stocks or bonds, quietly claim, "Infinite Intelligence governs and watches over all my financial transactions, and whatsoever I do shall prosper." Do this frequently and you will find that your investments will be wise; moreover you will be protected from loss, as you will be prompted to sell your securities or holdings before any loss accrues to you.

Let the following prayer be used daily by you regarding your home, business, and possessions: "The overshadowing Presence which guides the planets on their course and causes the sun to shine, watches over all my possessions, home, business, and all things that are mine. God is my fortress and vault. All my possessions are secure in God. It is wonderful." By reminding yourself daily of this great truth, and by observing the laws of Love, you will always be guided, watched over, and prospered in all your ways. You will never suffer from loss; for you have chosen the Most High as your Counsellor and Guide. The envelope of God's Love surrounds, enfolds, and encompasses you at all times. You rest in the Everlasting Arms of God.

All of us should seek an inner guidance for our problems. If you have a financial problem, repeat this before you retire at night: "Now I shall sleep in peace. I have turned this matter over to the God-Wisdom within. It knows only the answer. As the sun rises in the morning, so will my answer be resurrected. I know the sunrise never fails." Then go off to sleep.

Do not fret, fuss, and fume over a problem. Night brings counsel. Sleep on it. Your intellect can not solve all your problems. Pray for the Light that is to come. Remember the dawn always comes; then the shadows flee away. Let your sleep every night be a contented bliss.

You are not a victim of circumstances, except you believe you are. You can rise and overcome any circumstance or condition. You will have different experiences as you stand on the rock of spiritual Truth, steadfast, and faithful to your deeper purposes and desires.

In large stores, the management employs store detectives to prevent people from stealing; they catch a number every day trying to get something for nothing. All such people are living in the consciousness of lack and limitation, and are stealing from themselves, attracting at the same time all manner of loss. These people lack faith in God, and the understanding of how their minds work. If they would pray for true peace, Divine expression, and supply, they would find work; then by honesty, integrity, and perseverance they would become a credit to themselves and society at large.

Jesus said, "For ye have the poor always with you; but me ye have not always." The *poor states* of consciousness are always with us in this sense, that no matter how much wealth you now have, there is something you want with all your heart. It may be a problem of health; perhaps a son or daughter needs guidance, or harmony is lacking in the home. At that moment you are poor.

We could not know what abundance was, except we were conscious of lack. "I have chosen twelve, and one of you is a devil."

Whether it be the king of England or the boy in the slums, we are all born into limitation and into the race belief. It is through these limitations we grow. We could never discover the Inner Power, except through problems and difficulties; these are our *poor states* which prod us in seeking the solution. We could not know what joy was, except we could shed a tear of sorrow. We must be aware of poverty, to seek liberation and freedom, and ascend into God's opulence.

The *poor states*, such as fear, ignorance, worry, lack, and pain are not bad when they cause you to seek the opposite. When you get into trouble, and get kicked around from pillar to post; when you ask negative, heart-rending questions, such as "Why are all these things happening to me?" "Why does there seem to be a jinx following me?" light will come into your mind. Through your suffering, pain, or misery, you will discover the truth which sets you free. "Sweet are the uses of adversity, like a toad ugly and venomous, yet wears a precious jewel on its head."

Through dissatisfaction we are led to satisfaction. All those studying the laws of life have been dissatisfied with something. They have had some problem or difficulty which they could not solve; or they were not satisfied with the man-made answers to life's riddles. They have found their answer in the God-Presence within themselves—the pearl of great price—the precious jewel. The Bible says, "I sought the Lord, and I found him, and He delivered me from all my fears."

When you realize your ambition or desire, you will be satisfied for only a period of brief time; then the urge to expand will come again. This is Life seeking to express Itself at higher levels through you. When one desire is satisfied, another comes, etc. to infinity. You are here to grow. Life is progression; it is not static. You are here to go from glory to glory; there is no end; for there is no end to God's glory.

We are all poor in the sense we are forever seeking more light, wisdom, happiness, and greater joy out of life. God is Infinite, and never in Eternity could you exhaust the glory, beauty, and wisdom which is within; this is how wonderful you are.

In the absolute state all things are finished, but in the relative world we must awaken to that glory which was ours before the world was. No matter how wise you are, you are seeking more wisdom; so you are still poor. No matter how intelligent you are in the field of mathematics, physics, or astronomy, you are only scratching the surface. You are still poor. The journey is ever onward, upward, and Godward. It is really an awakening process, whereby you realize creation is finished. When you know God does not have to learn, grow, expand, or unfold, you begin to gradually awaken from the dream of limitation, and become alive in God. As the scales of fear, ignorance, race belief, and mass hypnosis fall from your eyes, you begin to see as God sees. The blind spots are removed; then you begin to see the world as God made it; for we begin to see it through God's eyes. Now you say, "Behold, the Kingdom of Heaven is at hand!"

Feed the "poor" within you; clothe the naked ideas, and give them form by believing in the reality of the idea, trusting the great Fabricator within to clothe it in form and objectify it. Now your word (idea) shall become flesh (take form). When you are hungry (poor states), you seek food. When worried, you seek peace. When you are sick, you seek health; when you are weak, you seek strength. Your desire for prosperity is the voice of God in you telling you that abundance is yours; therefore, through your poor state, you find the urge to grow, to expand, to unfold, to achieve, and to accomplish your desires.

A pain in your shoulder is a blessing in disguise; it tells you to do something about it at once. If there were no pain and no indication of trouble, your arm might fall off on the street. Your pain is God's alarm system telling you to seek His Peace and His Healing Power, and move from darkness to Light. When cold, you build a fire. When you are hungry, you eat. When you are in lack, enter into the mood of opulence and plenty. Imagine the end; rejoice in it. Having imagined the end, and felt it as true, you have willed the means to the realization of the end.

When you are fearful and worried, feed your mind with the great truths of God that have stood the test of time and will last forever. You can receive comfort by meditating on the great psalms. For example: "The Lord is my shepherd; I shall not want." "God is my refuge, my salvation, whom shall I fear?" "God is an ever-present help in time of trouble." "My God in Him will I trust." "He shall cover me with His feathers, and under His wings shall I rest." "One with God is a majority." "If God be for me, who can be against me?" "I do all things through Christ which strengtheneth me." Let the healing vibrations of these truths flood your mind and heart; then you will crowd out of your mind all your fears, doubts, and worries through this meditative process.

Imbibe another great spiritual truth: "A merry heart maketh a cheerful countenance." "A merry heart hath a continual feast." "A merry heart doeth good like a medicine; a broken spirit drieth the bones." "Therefore I put thee in remembrance that thou stir up the gift of God within thee." Begin *now* to stir up the gift of

God by completely rejecting the evidence of senses, the tyranny and despotism of the race mind, and give complete recognition to the spiritual Power within you as the only Cause, the only Power, and the only Presence. Know that it is a responsive and beneficent Power. "Draw nigh unto it, and it will draw nigh unto you." Turn to It devotedly with assurance, trust, and love; it will respond to you as love, peace, guidance, and prosperity.

It will be your Comforter, Guide, Counsellor, and your heavenly Father. You will then say, "God is Love. I have found Him, and He truly has delivered me from all my fears." Furthermore, you will find yourself in green pastures, where abundance and all of God's riches flow freely through you.

Say to yourself freely and joyously during the day, "I walk in the consciousness of the Presence of God all day long." "His fulness flows through me at all times filling up all the empty vessels in my life."

When you are filled full of the feeling of being what you long to be, your prayer is answered. Are all the vessels full in your life? Look under health, wealth, love, and expression. Are you fully satisfied on all levels? Is there something lacking in one of these four? All that you seek, no matter what it is, comes under one of these classifications.

If you say, "All I want is truth or wisdom," you are expressing the desire of all men everywhere. That is what everyone wants, even though he or she may word it differently. Truth or wisdom is the overall desire of every man; this comes under the classification of expression. You wish to express more and more of God here and now.

Through your lack, limitation, and problems, you grow in God's Light, and you discover yourself. There is no other way whereby you could discover yourself.

If you could not use your powers two ways, you would never discover yourself; neither would you ever deduce a law governing you. If you were compelled to be good, or compelled to love, that would not be love. You would then be an automaton. You have freedom to love, because you can give it, or retain it. If compelled to love, there is no love. Aren't you flattered when some woman tells you she loves you and wants you? She has chosen you from all the men in the world. She does not have to love you. If she were forced to love you, you would not be flattered or happy about it.

You have freedom to be a murderer or a Holy man. This is the reason that we praise such men as Lincoln and others. They decided to choose the good; we praise them for their choice. If we believe that circumstances, conditions, events, age, race, religious training, or early environment can preclude the possibility of our attaining a happy, prosperous life, we are thieves and robbers. All that is necessary to express happiness and prosperity is to *feel* happy and prosperous. The feeling of wealth produces wealth. States of consciousness manifest themselves. This is why it is said, "All that ever came before me (feeling) are thieves and robbers." Feeling is the law, and the law is the feeling.

Your desire for prosperity is really the promise of God saying that His riches are yours; accept this promise without any mental reservation.

Quimby likened prayer to that of a lawyer pleading the case before the judge. This teacher of the laws of mind said he could prove the defendant was not guilty as charged, but that the person was a victim of lies and false beliefs. You are the judge; you render your own verdict; then you are set free. The negative thoughts of lack, poverty, and failure are all false; they are all lies; there is nothing to back them up.

You know there is only one spiritual Power, one primal cause, and you, therefore, cease giving power to conditions, circumstances, and opinions of men. Give all Power to the Spiritual Power within you, knowing that It will respond to your thought of abundance and prosperity. Recognizing the supremacy of the

Spirit within, and the Power of your own thought or mental image is the way to opulence, freedom, and constant supply. Accept the abundant life in your own mind. Your mental acceptance and expectancy of wealth has its own mathematics and mechanics of expression. As you enter into the mood of opulence, all things necessary for the abundant life will come to pass. You are now the judge arriving at a decision in the courthouse of your mind. You have, like Quimby, produced indisputable evidence showing how the laws of your mind work, and you are now free from fear. You have executed and chopped the heads off all the fear and superstitious thoughts in your mind. Fear is the signal for action; it is not really bad; it tells you to move to the opposite which is faith in God and all positive values.

Let this be your daily prayer; write it in your heart: "God is the source of my supply. That supply is my supply now. His riches flow to me freely, copiously, and abundantly. I am forever conscious of my true worth. I give of my talents freely, and I am wonderfully, divinely compensated. Thank you, Father!"

2

The Road To Riches

Riches are of the mind. Let us suppose for a moment that a physician's diploma was stolen together with his office equipment. I am sure you would agree that his wealth was in his mind.

He could still carry on, diagnose disease, prescribe, operate, and lecture on materia medica. Only his symbols were stolen; he could always get additional supplies. His riches were in his mental capacity, knowledge to help others, and his ability to contribute to humanity in general.

You will always be wealthy when you have an intense desire to contribute to the good of mankind. Your urge for service—i.e., to give of your talents to the world—will always find a response in the heart of the universe.

I knew a man in New York during the financial crisis of 1929, who lost everything he had including his home and all his life's savings. I met him after a lecture which I had given at one of the hotels in the city. This was what he said: "I lost everything. I made a million dollars in four years. I will make it again. All I have lost is a symbol. I can again attract the symbol of wealth in the same way as honey attracts flies."

I followed the career of this man for several years to discover the key to his success. The key may seem strange to you; yet it is a very old one. The name he gave the key was, "Change water into wine!" He read this passage in the Bible, and he knew it was the answer to perfect health, happiness, peace of mind, and prosperity.

Wine in the Bible always means the realization of your desires, urges, plans, dreams, propositions, etc.; in other words, it is the things you wish to accomplish, achieve, and bring forth.

Water in the Bible usually refers to your mind or consciousness. Water takes the shape of any vessel into which it is poured; likewise whatever you feel and believe as true will become manifest in your world; thus you are always changing water into wine.

The Bible was written by illumined men; it teaches practical, everyday psychology and a way of life. One of the cardinal tenets of the Bible is that you determine, mold, fashion, and shape your own destiny through right thought, feeling, and beliefs. It teaches you that you can solve any problem, overcome any situation, and that you are born to succeed, to win, and to triumph. In order to discover the Royal Road to Riches, and receive the strength and security necessary to advance in life, you must cease viewing the Bible in the traditional way.

The above man who was in a financial crisis used to say to himself frequently during the days when he was without funds, "I can change water into wine!" These words meant to him, "I can exchange the poverty ideas in my mind for the realization of my present desires or needs which are wealth and financial supply."

His mental attitude (water) was, "Once I made a fortune honestly. I will make it again [wine]." His regular affirmation consisted of, "I attracted the symbol [money] once, I am attracting it again. I know this, and feel it is true [wine]."

This man went to work as a salesman for a chemical organization. Ideas for the better promotion of their products came to him; he passed them on to his organization. It was not long until he became vice president. Within four years the company made him president. His constant mental attitude was, "I can change water into wine!"

Look upon the story in John of changing water into wine in a figurative way, and say to yourself as the above-mentioned chemical salesman did: "I can make the invisible ideas, urges, dreams, and desires of mine visible, because I have discovered a simple, universal law of mind."

The law he demonstrated is the law of action and reaction. It means your external world, body, circumstances, environment, and financial status are always a perfect reflection of your inner thinking, beliefs, feelings, and convictions. This being true, you can now change your inner pattern of thought by dwelling on the idea of success, wealth, and peace of mind. As you busy your mind with these latter concepts, these ideas will gradually seep into your mentality like seeds planted in the ground. As all seeds (thoughts and ideas) grow after their kind, so will your habitual thinking and feeling manifest in prosperity, success, and peace of mind. Wise thought (action) is followed by right action (reaction).

You can acquire riches when you become aware of the fact that prayer is a marriage feast. The *feast* is a psychological one; you meditate (mentally eat of) on your good or your desire until you become *one* with it.

I will now cite a case history from my files relating how a young girl performed her first miracle in transforming "water into wine." She operated a very beautiful hair salon. Her mother became ill, and she had to devote considerable time at home neglecting her business. During her absence two of her assistants embezzled funds. She was forced into bankruptcy, losing her home and finding herself deeply in debt. She was unable to pay hospital bills for her mother, and she was now unemployed.

I explained to this woman the magic formula of changing water into wine. Again we made it clear to her that *wine* means answered prayer or the objectification of her ideal.

She was quarreling with the outside world. She said, "Look at the facts: I have lost everything; it is a cruel world. I cannot pay my bills. I do not pray; for I have lost hope." She was so absorbed and engrossed in the material world, that she was completely oblivious to the internal cause of her situation. As we talked, she began to understand that she had to resolve the quarrel in her mind.

No matter what your desire or ideal is as you read this book, you will also find some thought or idea in your mind opposed to it. For example your desire may be for health; perhaps there are several thoughts such as these in your mind simultaneously: "I can't be healed. I have tried, but it is no use; it's getting worse." "I don't know enough about spiritual mind healing."

As you study yourself, don't you have a tug of war in your mind? Like this girl, you find environment and external affairs challenging your desire of expression, wealth, and peace of mind.

True prayer is a mental marriage feast, and it teaches us all how to resolve the mental conflict. In prayer you "write" what you *believe* in your own mind. Emerson said, "A man is what he thinks all day long." By your habitual thinking you make your own mental laws of belief. By repeating a certain train of thought you establish definite opinions and beliefs in the deeper mind called the subconscious; then such mental acceptances, beliefs, and opinions direct and control all the outer actions. To understand this and begin to apply it is the first step in changing "water into wine," or changing lack and limitation into abundance and opulence. The man who is unaware of his own inner, spiritual powers is, therefore, subject to race beliefs, lack, and limitation.

Open your Bible now, and perform your first miracle, as this beauty operator did. You can do it. If you merely read the Bible as a historical event, you will miss the spiritual, mental, scientific view of the laws of mind with which we are concerned in this book.

Let us take this passage: "And the third day there was a marriage in Cana of Galilea; and the mother of Jesus was there." *Galilee* means your mind or consciousness. *Cana* means your desire. The *marriage* is purely mental or the subjective embodiment of your desire. This whole, beautiful drama of prayer is a psychological one in which all the characters are mental states, feelings, and ideas within you.

One of the meanings of *Jesus* is illumined reason. The *mother of Jesus* means the feeling, moods, or emotions which possess us.

"And both Jesus was called, and his disciples, to the marriage." Your *disciples* are your inner powers and faculties enabling you to realize your desires.

"And when they wanted wine, the mother of Jesus saith unto him, They have no wine." *Wine*, as we have stated, represents the answered prayer or the manifestation of your desire and ideals in life. You can now see this is an everyday drama taking place in your own life.

When you wish to accomplish something as this girl did, namely, finding work, supply, and a way out of your problem, suggestions of lack come to you; such as, "There is no hope. All is lost, I can't accomplish it; it is hopeless." This is the voice from the outside world saying to you, "They have no wine," or "Look at the facts." This is your feeling of lack, limitation, or bondage speaking.

How do you meet the challenge of circumstances and conditions? By now you are getting acquainted with the laws of mind which are as follows: "As I think and feel inside, so is my outside world; i.e., my body, finances, environment, social position, and all phases of my external relationship to the world and man." Your internal, mental movements and imagery govern, control, and direct the external plane in your life.

The Bible says, "As he thinketh in his heart, so *is* he." The *heart* is a Chaldean word meaning the subconscious mind. In other words your thought must reach subjective levels by engaging the power of your subliminal self.

Thought and feeling are your destiny. Thought charged with feeling and interest is always subjectified, and becomes manifest in your world. *Prayer* is a marriage of thought and feeling, or your idea and emotion; this is what the marriage feast relates.

Any idea or desire of the mind felt as true comes to pass, whether it is good, bad, or indifferent. Knowing the law now that what you imagine and feel in your mind, you will express, manifest, or experience in the outside, enables you to begin to discipline your mind.

When the suggestion of lack, fear, doubt, or despair (they have no wine) come to your mind, immediately reject it mentally by focusing your attention at once on the answered prayer, or the fulfillment of your desire.

The statement given in the Bible from John 2, "Mine hour is not yet come," and "Woman, what have I to do with thee," are figurative, idiomatic, oriental expressions.

As we paraphrase this quotation, *woman* means the negative feeling that you indulge in. These negative suggestions have no power or reality, because there is nothing to back them up.

A suggestion of lack has no power; the power is resident in your own thought and feeling.

What does God mean to you? *God* is the Name given to the One Spiritual Power. *God* is the One Invisible Source from Which all things flow.

When your thoughts are constructive and harmonious, the spiritual power being responsive to your thought flows as harmony, health, and abundance. Practice the wonderful discipline of completely rejecting every thought of lack by immediately recognizing the availability of the spiritual power, and its response to your constructive thoughts and imagery; then you will be practicing the truth found in these words, "Woman what have I to do with thee?"

We read, "Mine hour is not yet come." This means that while you have not yet reached a conviction or positive state of mind, you know you are on the way mentally, because you are engaging your mind on the positive ideals, goals, and objectives in life. Whatever the mind dwells upon, it multiplies, magnifies, and causes it to grow until finally the mind becomes qualified with the new state of consciousness. You are then conditioned positively, whereas before you were conditioned negatively.

The spiritual man in prayer moves from the mood of lack to the mood of confidence, peace, and trust in the spiritual power within himself. Since his trust and faith are in the Spiritual Power, his mother (moods and feeling) registers a feeling of triumph or victory; this will bring about the solution or the answer to your prayer.

The waterpots in the story from the Bible refer to the mental cycles that man goes through in order to bring about the subjective realization of his desire. The length of time may be a moment, hour, week, or month depending on the faith and state of consciousness of the student.

In prayer we must cleanse our mind of false beliefs, fear, doubt, and anxiety by becoming completely detached from the evidence of senses and the external world. In the peacefulness and quietude of your mind, wherein you have stilled the wheels of your mind, meditate on the joy of the answered prayer until that inner certitude comes, whereby *you know that you know*. When you have succeeded in being *one* with your desire, you have succeeded in the mental marriage—or the union of your feeling with your idea.

I am sure you wish to be married (one with) to health, harmony, success, and achievement in your mind at this moment. Every time you pray you are trying to perform the *marriage feast of Cana* (realization of your desire or ideas). You want to be mentally identified with the concept of peace, success, well being, and perfect health.

"They filled them up to the brim." *The six waterpots* represent your own mind in the spiritual and mental creative act. You must fill your mind *to the brim*, meaning you must become filled full of the feeling of being what you long to be. When you succeed in filling your mind with the ideal you wish to accomplish or express, you are full to the brim; then you cease praying about it; for you feel its reality in your mind. You *know!* It is a finished state of consciousness. You are at peace about it.

"And he saith unto them Draw out now, and bear unto the governor of the feast." Whatever is impregnated in our subconscious mind is always objectified on the screen of space; consequently when we enter a state of conviction that our prayer is answered, we have given the command, "Bear unto the governor of the feast."

You are always governing your mental feast. During the day thousands of thoughts, suggestions, opinions, sights, and sounds reach your eyes and ears. You can reject them as unfit for mental consumption or entertain them as you choose. Your conscious, reasoning, intellectual mind is the governor of the feast. When you consciously choose to entertain, meditate, feast upon, and imagine your heart's desire as true, it becomes a living embodiment, and a part of your mentality, so that your deeper self gives birth or expression to it. In other words what is impressed subjectively is expressed objectively. Your senses or conscious mind sees the objectification of your good. When the conscious mind becomes aware of "water made into wine," it becomes aware of the answered prayer. Water might be called, also, the invisible, formless, spiritual power, unconditioned consciousness. Wine is conditioned consciousness, or the mind giving birth to its beliefs and convictions.

The servants which draw the water for you represent the mood of peace, confidence, and faith. According to your faith or feeling, your good is attracted or drawn to you.

Imbibe, cherish, fall in love with these spiritual principles which are discussed in this book. In the first recorded miracle of Jesus, you are told that prayer is a marriage feast, or the mind uniting with its desire.

Love is the fulfilling of the law. Love is really an emotional attachment, a sense of oneness with your good. You must be true to that which you love. You must be loyal to your purpose or to your ideal. We are not being true to the one we love, when we are flirting of mentally entertaining other marriages with fear, doubt, worry, anxiety, or false beliefs. Love is a state of oneness, a state of fulfillment. (Refer to the book by the author, *Love is Freedom*.)

When this simple drama was explained to the beauty operator mentioned about, she became rich mentally. She understood this drama, and she put it into practice in her life. This is how she prayed:

She knew that the *water* (her own mind) would flow, and fill up all the *empty vessels* in response to her new way of thinking and feeling.

At night this client became very quiet and still, relaxed her body, and began to use constructive imagery. The steps she used are as follows:

First step: She began to imagine the local bank manager was congratulating her on her wonderful deposits in the bank. She kept imagining that for about five minutes.

The second step: In her imagination she heard her mother saying to her, "I am so happy about your wonderful, new position."

She continued to hear her say this in a happy, joyous way for about three to five minutes.

The third step: Vividly she imagined the writer was in front of her performing her marriage ceremony. This woman heard me saying as the officiating minister, "I now pronounce you man and wife." Completing this routine, she went off to sleep feeling filled full, i.e., sensing and feeling within herself the joy of the answered prayer.

Nothing happened for three weeks; in fact things got much worse, but she persevered, refusing to take "No" for her answer. She knew that in order to grow spiritually, she too, had to perform her first miracle by changing her fear to faith, her mood of lack to a mood of opulence and prosperity, by changing consciousness (water) into the conditions, circumstances, and experiences she wished to express.

Consciousness, Awareness, Beingness, Principle, Spirit, or whatever Name you give It is the cause of all; it is the only Presence and Power. The Spiritual Power of Spirit within us is the cause and substance of all things. All things—birds, trees, stars, sun, moon, earth, gold, silver, and platinum—are its manifestations. It is the cause and substance of all things. "There is none else."

Understanding this she knew that *water* (consciousness) could become supply in the form of money, true place, or true expression for herself, health for her mother, as well as companionship and fullness of life. She saw this simple—yet profound—truth in the twinkling of an eye, and said to me, "I *accept* my good."

She knew that nothing is hidden from us; all of God is within us, waiting for our discovery and inquiry.

In less than a month this young girl got married. The writer performed the ceremony. I pronounced the words she heard me say over and over again in her meditative, relaxed state, "I now pronounce you man and wife!"

Her husband gave her a check for $24,000 as a wedding present, as well as a trip around the world. Her new expression as a beauty operator was to beautify her home and garden, and make the desert of her mind rejoice and blossom as the rose.

She changed "water into wine." *Water* or her consciousness became charged or conditioned by her constant, true, happy imagery. These images, when sustained regularly, systematically, and with faith in the developing powers of the deeper mind, will come out of the darkness (subconscious mind) into light (objectified on the screen of space).

There is one important rule: Do not expose this newly developed film to the shattering light of fear, doubt, despondency, and worry. Whenever worry or fear knocks at your door, immediately turn to the picture you developed in your mind, and say to yourself, "A beautiful picture is being developed now in the dark house of my mind." Mentally pour on that picture your feeling of joy, faith, and understanding. You know you have operated a psychological, spiritual law; for what is impressed shall be expressed. It is wonderful!

The following is a sure, certain way for developing and manifesting all the material riches and supply you need all the days of your life. If you apply this formula sincerely and honestly, you should be amply rewarded on the external plane. I will illustrate this by telling you of a man who came to see me in London in desperate financial straits. He was a member of the Church of England, and had studied the working of the subconscious mind to some extent.

I told him to say frequently during the day, "God is the source of my supply, and all my needs are met at every moment of time and point of space." Think also of all the animal life in this world, and in all the galaxies of space which are now being taken care of by an Infinite Intelligence. Notice how nature is lavish, extravagant, and bountiful. Think of the fish of the sea which are all being sustained, as well as the birds of the air!"

He began to realize that since he was born, he had been taken care of; fed by his mother; clothed by his father, and watched over by tender, loving parents. This man got a job and was paid in a wonderful way. He reasoned that it was illogical to assume that the Principle of Life which gave him life, and always took care of him would suddenly cease to respond to him.

He realized that he had cut off his own supply by resenting his employer, self-condemnation, criticism of himself, and by his own sense of unworthiness. He had psychologically severed the cord which joined him to the Infinite Source of all things—the Indwelling Spirit or Life Principle, called by some "Consciousness or Awareness."

Man is not fed like the birds; he must consciously commune with the Indwelling Power and Presence, and receive guidance, strength, vitality, and all things necessary for the fulfillment of his needs. This is the formula which he used to change water into the wine of abundance and financial success. He realized God or the Spiritual Power within him was the cause of all; furthermore he realized that if he could sell himself the idea that wealth was his by Divine right, he would manifest abundance of supply.

The affirmation he used was, "God is the source of my supply. All my financial and other needs are met at every moment of time and point of space; there is always a divine surplus." This simple statement repeated frequently, knowingly, and intelligently conditioned his mind to a prosperity consciousness.

All he had to do was to sell himself this positive idea, in the same way a good salesman has to sell himself on the merits of his product. Such a person is convinced of the integrity of his company, the high quality of the product, the good service which it will give the customer, and the fact that the price is right, etc.

I told him whenever negative thoughts came to his mind, which would happen, not to fight them, quarrel with them in any way, but simply go back to the spiritual, mental formula, and repeat it quietly and lovingly to himself. Negative thoughts came to him in avalanches at times in the form of a flood of negativity. Each time he met them with the positive, firm, loyal conviction: "God supplies all my needs; there is a Divine surplus in my life."

He said as he drove his car, and went through his day's routine, that a host of sundry, miscellaneous, negative concepts crowded his mind from time to time; such as, "There is no hope." "You are broke." Each time such negative thoughts came, he refused their mental admission by turning to the Eternal Source of wealth, health, and all things which he knew to be his own spiritual awareness. Definitely and positively he claimed, "God is the source of my supply, and that supply is mine now!" Or, "There is a Divine solution. God's wealth is my wealth," and other affirmative, positive statements which charged his mind with hope, faith, expectancy, and ultimately a conviction in an ever-flowing fountain of riches supplying all his needs copiously, joyously, and endlessly.

The negative flood of thoughts came to him as often as fifty times in an hour; each time he refused to open the door of his mind to these gangsters, assassins, and thieves which he knew would only rob him of peace, wealth, success, and all good things. Instead he opened the door of his mind to the idea of God's Eternal Life Principle of supply flowing through him as wealth, health, energy, power, and all things necessary to lead a full and happy life here.

As he continued to do this, the second day not so many thieves knocked at his door; the third day, the flow of negative visitors was less; the fourth day, they came intermittently, hoping for admission, but receiving the same mental response: "No entrance! I accept only thoughts and concepts which activate, heal, bless, and inspire my mind!"

He reconditioned his consciousness or mind to a wealth consciousness. "The prince of this world cometh, and hath nothing in me"—This conveys to your mind: The negative thoughts, such as, fear, lack, worry, anxiety came, but they received no response from his mind. He was now immune; God intoxicated, and seized by a divine faith in an ever-expanding consciousness of abundance and financial supply. This man did not lose everything; neither did he go into bankruptcy; he was given extended credit; his business improved; new doors opened up, and he prospered.

Remember always in the prayer-process, you must be loyal to your ideal, purpose, and objective. Many people fail to realize wealth and financial success, because they pray two ways. They affirm God is their supply, and that they are divinely prospered, but a few minutes later they deny their good by saying, "I can't pay this bill." "I can't afford this, that, or the other things." Or they say to themselves, "A jinx is following me." "I can't ever make ends meet." "I never have enough to go around." All such statements are highly destructive, and neutralize your positive prayers. This is what is called, "praying two ways."

You must be faithful to your plan or your goal. You must be true to your knowledge of the spiritual power. Cease making negative marriages, i.e., uniting with negative thoughts, fears, and worries.

Prayer is like a captain directing the course of his ship. You must have a destination. You must know where you are going. The captain of the ship, knowing the laws of navigation, regulates his course accordingly. If the ship is turned from its course by storms or unruly waves, he calmly redirects it along its true course.

You are the captain on the bridge, and you are giving the orders in the way of thoughts, feelings, opinions, beliefs, moods, and mental tones. Keep your eye on the beam. *You go where your vision is!*

Cease, therefore, looking at all the obstacles, delays, and impediments that would cause you to go off your course. Be definite and positive. Decide where you are going. Know that your mental attitude is the ship which will take you from the mood of lack and limitation, to the mood and feeling of opulence, and to the belief in the inevitable law of God working for you.

Quimby, who was a doctor, a wonderful student, and teacher of the mental and spiritual laws of mind, said, "Man acts as he is acted upon." What moves you now? What is it that determines your response to life? The answer is as follows: Your ideas, beliefs, and opinions activate your mind and condition you to the point that you become, as Quimby stated, "An expression of your beliefs." This illustrates the truth of Quimby's statement: "Man is belief expressed."

Another popular statement of Quimby's was, "Our minds mingle like atmospheres, and each person has his identity in that atmosphere." When you were a child, you were subject to the moods, feelings, beliefs, and the general mental atmosphere of the home. The fears, anxieties, superstitions, as well as the religious faith and convictions of the parents were impressed on your mind.

Let us say the child had been brought up in a poverty-stricken home, in which there was never enough to go around, financially speaking; he heard constantly the complaint of lack and limitation. You could say, like Salter in his conditioned reflex therapy, that the child was conditioned to poverty. The young man may have a poverty complex based on his early experiences, training, and beliefs, but he can rise above any situation, and become free; this is done through the power of prayer.

I knew a young boy aged 17, who was born in a place called Hell's Kitchen, in New York. He listened to some lectures I was giving in Steinway Hall, New York, at the time. This boy realized that he had been the victim of negative, destructive thinking, and that if he did not redirect his mind along constructive channels, the world-mind with its fears, failures, hates, and jealousies would move in and control him. "Man acts as he is acted upon."

It stands to reason, as Quimby knew, that if man will not take charge of his own house (mind), the propaganda, false beliefs, fears, and worries of the phenomenalistic world will act as a hypnotic spell over him.

We are immersed in the race mind which believes in sickness, death, misfortune, accident, failures, disease, and diverse disasters. Follow the Biblical injunction: "Come out from among them, and be separate." Identify yourself mentally and emotionally with the Eternal Verities which have stood the test of time.

This young man decided to think and plan for himself. He decided to take the Royal Road to Riches by accepting God's abundance here and now, and to fill his mind with spiritual concepts and perceptions. He knew, as he did this, he would automatically crowd out of his mind all negative patterns.

He adopted a simple process called, "scientific imagination." He had a wonderful voice, but it was not cultivated or developed. I told him the image he gave attention to in his mind would be developed in his deeper mind and come to pass. He understood this to be a law of mind—a law of action and reaction—i.e., the response of the deeper mind to the mental picture held in the conscious mind.

This young man would sit down quietly in his room at home; relax his whole body, and vividly imagine himself singing before a microphone. He would actually reach out for the "feel" of the instrument. He would hear me congratulate him on his wonderful contract, and tell him how magnificent his voice was. By giving his attention and devotion to this mental image regularly and systematically, a deep impression was made on his subconscious mind.

A short time elapsed, and an Italian voice instructor in New York gave him free lessons several times a week, because he saw his possibilities. He got a contract which sent him abroad to sing in the salons of Europe, Asia, South Africa, and other places. His financial worries were over; for he also received a wonderful salary. His hidden talents and ability to release them were his real riches. These talents and powers within all of us are God-given; let us release them.

Did you ever say to yourself, "How can I be more useful to my fellow creature?" "How can I contribute more to humanity?"

A minister-friend of mine told me that in his early days he and his church suffered financially. His technique or process was this simple prayer which worked wonders for him, "God reveals to me better ways to present the truths of God to my fellow creature." Money poured in; the mortgage was paid in a few years, and he has never worried about money since.

As you read this chapter, you have now learned that the inner feelings, moods, and beliefs of man always control and govern his external world. The inner movements of the mind control the outer movements. To change the outside, you must change the inside. "As in Heaven, so on earth;" or as in my mind or consciousness, so is it in my body, circumstances, and environment.

The Bible says, "There is nothing hidden that shall not be revealed." For example if you are sick, you are revealing a mental and emotional pattern which is the cause. If you are upset, or if you receive tragic news, notice how you reveal it in your face, eyes, gestures, tonal qualities, also in your gait and posture. As a matter of fact your whole body reveals your inner distress. You could, of course, through mental discipline and prayer, remain absolutely poised, serene, and calm, refusing to betray your hidden feelings or mental states. You could order the muscles of your body to relax, be quiet, and be still; they would have to obey you. Your eyes, face, and lips would not betray any sign of grief, anger, or despondency. On the other hand with a little discipline, through prayer and meditation, you could reverse the entire picture. Even though you had received disturbing news, regardless of its grave nature, you could show and exhibit joy, peace, relaxation, and a vibrant, buoyant nature. No one would ever know that you were the recipient of so-called bad news.

Regardless of what kind of news you received today, you could go to the mirror, look at your face, lips, eyes, and your gestures, as you tell yourself, and imagine you have heard the news of having received a vast fortune. Dramatize it, feel it, thrill to it, and notice how your whole body responds to the inner thrill.

You can reverse any situation through prayer. Busy your mind with the concepts of peace, success, wealth, and happiness. Identify yourself with these ideas mentally, emotionally, and pictorially.

Get a picture of yourself as you want to be; retain that image; sustain it with joy, faith, and expectancy; finally you will succeed in experiencing its manifestation.

I say to people who consult me regarding financial lack to "marry wealth." Some see the point, others do not. As all Bible students know, your *wife* is what you are mentally joined to, united with, or at one with.

In other words what you conceive and believe, you give it conception. If you believe the world is cold, cruel, and harsh, that it is a "dog eat dog" way of life, that is *your* concept; you are married to it, and you will have children or issue by that marriage. The children from such a mental marriage or belief will be your experiences, conditions, and circumstances together with all other events in your life. All your experiences and reactions to life will be the image and likeness of the ideas which fathered them.

Look at the many wives the average man is living with, such as fear, doubt, anxiety, criticism, jealousy, and anger; these play havoc with his mind. Marry wealth by claiming, feeling, and believing: "God supplies all my needs according to his riches in glory." Or take the following statement, and repeat it over and over again knowingly until your consciousness is conditioned by it, or it becomes a part of your meditation: "I am divinely expressed, and I have a wonderful income." Do not say this in a parrot-like fashion, but know that your train of thought is being engraved in your deeper mind, and it becomes a conditioned state of consciousness. Let the phrase become meaningful to you. Pour life, love, and feeling on it, making it alive.

One of my class-students recently opened a restaurant. He phoned me saying that he got married to a restaurant; he meant that he had made up his mind to be very successful, diligent, and persevering, and to see that his business prospered. This man's *wife* (mental) was his belief in the accomplishment of his desire or wish.

Identify yourself with your aim in life, and cease mental marriages with criticism, self-condemnation, anger, fear, and worry. Give attention to your chosen ideal, being full of faith and confidence in the inevitable law of prosperity and success. You will accomplish nothing by loving your ideal one minute, and denying it the next minute; this is like mixing acid and an alkali; for you will get an inert substance. In going along the Royal Road to Riches, you must be faithful to your chosen ideal (your wife).

We find illustrations in the Bible relating to these same truths. For instance, "Eve came out of Adam's rib." *Your rib* is your concept, desire, idea, plan, goal, or aim in life.

Eve means the emotion, feeling nature, or the inner tone. In other words you must mother the idea. The idea must be mothered, loved, and felt as true, in order to manifest your aim in life.

The *idea* is the father; the *emotion* is the mother; this is the marriage feast which is always taking place in your mind.

Ouspensky spoke of the third element which entered in or was formed following the union of your desire and feeling. He called it the neutral element. We may call it "peace"; for God is Peace.

The Bible says, "And the government shall be on his shoulders." In other words let Divine Wisdom be your guide. Let the subjective Wisdom within you lead, guide, and govern you in all your ways. Turn over your request to this Indwelling Presence knowing in your heart and soul that it will dissipate the anxiety, heal the wound, and restore your soul to equanimity and tranquility. Open your mind and heart, and say, "God is my pilot. He leads me. He prospers me. He is my counsellor." Let your prayer be night and morning, "I am a channel through which God's riches flow ceaselessly, copiously, and freely." Write that prayer in your heart, inscribe it in your mind. Keep on the beam of God's glory!

The man who does not know the inner workings of his own mind is full of burdens, anxieties, and worries; for he has not learned how to cast his burden on the Indwelling Presence, and go free. The Zen monk was asked by his disciple, "What is Truth?" He replied in a symbolic way by taking the bag off his back, and placing it on the ground.

The disciple then asked him, "Master, how does it work?"

The Zen monk still silent, placed the bag on his back, and walked on down the road singing to himself. The *bag* is your burden, or your problem. You cast it on the subjective Wisdom which knows all, and has the "know-how" of accomplishment. It knows only the answer.

Placing the bag again on his back means though I still have the problem, I now have mental rest and relief from the burden, because I have invoked the Divine Wisdom on my behalf; therefore I sing the song of triumph, knowing that the answer to my prayer is on the way, and I sing for the joy that is set before me. It is wonderful.

"Every man at the beginning doth set forth good wine; and when men have well drunk, then that which is worse; but thou hast kept the good wine until now." This is true of every man when he first enters a knowledge of the laws of mind. He sets out with high spirits and ambitions. He is the new broom which sweeps clean, and he is full of good intentions; oftentimes he forgets the Source of power. He does not remain faithful to the Principle within him, which is scientific and effectual, that would lift him out of his negative experiences, and set him on the high road to freedom and peace of mind. He begins to indulge mentally and emotionally with ideas and thoughts extraneous to his announced aim and goal. In other words he is not faithful to his ideal or wife.

Know that the subjective or deeper self within you will accept your request, and being the great fabricator, it will bring it to pass in its own way. All you do is release your request with faith and confidence, in the same way you would cast a seed on the ground, or mail a letter to a friend, knowing the answer would come.

Did you ever go between two great rocks and listen to the echo of your voice? This is the way the Life Principle within you answers. *You* will hear the echo of your own voice. Your *voice* is your inner, mental movement of the mind—your inner, psychological journey where you feasted mentally on an idea until you were full; then you rested.

Knowing this law and how to use it, be sure you never become drunk with power, arrogance, pride, or conceit. Use the law to bless, heal, inspire, and lift up others, as well as yourself.

Man misuses the law by selfishly taking advantage of his fellow man; if you do, you hurt and attract loss to yourself. Power, security, and riches are not to be obtained externally. They come from the treasure-house of eternity within. We should realize that the *good wine* is always present, for God is the Eternal Now. Regardless of present circumstances, you can prove your good is ever-present by detaching yourself mentally from the problem, going on the High Watch, and go about your Father's business.

To go on the High Watch is to envision your good, to dwell on the new concept of yourself, to become married to it, and sustain the happy mood by remaining faithful—full of faith every step of the way—knowing that the wine of joy, the answered prayer, is on the way. "Now is the day of salvation." "The kingdom of heaven is at hand." "Thou hast kept the good wine until now."

You can—this moment—travel psychologically in your mind, and enter mentally through divine imagination into any desired state. The wealth, health, or invention you wish to introduce are all invisible first. Everything comes out of the Invisible. You must subjectively possess riches, before you can objectively possess wealth. The feeling of wealth produces wealth; for wealth is a state of consciousness. *A state of consciousness* is how you think, feel, believe, and what you mentally give consent to.

A teacher in California receiving over five or six thousand dollars a year looked in a window at a beautiful ermine coat that was priced at $8,000. She said, "It would take me years to save that amount of money. I could never afford it. Oh, how I want it!" She listened to our lectures on Sunday mornings. By ceasing to marry these negative concepts, she learned that she could have a coat, car, or anything she wished without hurting anybody on the face of the earth.

I told her to imagine she had the coat on, to feel its beautiful fur, and to get the feel of it on her. She began to use the power of her imagination prior to sleep at night. She put the imaginary coat on her, fondled it, caressed it, like a child does with her doll. She continued to do this, and finally felt the thrill of it all.

She went to sleep every night wearing this imaginary coat, and being so happy in possessing it. Three months went by, and nothing happened. She was about to waver, but she reminded herself that it is the sustained mood which demonstrates. "He who perseveres to the end shall be saved." The solution will come to the person who does not waver, but always goes about with the *perfume of His Presence* with him. The answer comes to the man who walks in the light that "It is done!" You are always using the perfume of His Presence when you sustain the happy, joyous mood of expectancy knowing your good is on the way. You saw it on the unseen, and you *know* you will see it in the seen.

The sequel to the teacher's drama of the mind is interesting. One Sunday morning after our lecture, a man accidentally stepped on her toe, apologized profusely, asked her where she lived, and offered to drive her home. She accepted gladly. Shortly after he proposed marriage; gave her a beautiful diamond ring, and said to her, "I saw the most wonderful coat; you would simply look radiant wearing it!" It was the coat she admired three months previously. (The salesman said over one hundred wealthy women looked at the coat, admired it immensely, but for some reason always selected another garment.)

Through your capacity to choose, imagine the reality of what you have selected, and through faith and perseverance, *you can* realize your goal in life. All the riches of heaven are here now within you waiting to be released. Peace, joy, love, guidance, inspiration, goodwill, and abundance all exist now. All that is necessary in order to express God's riches is for you to leave the present now (your limitation), enter into the mental vision or picture, and in a happy, joyous mood become one with your ideal. Having seen and felt your good in moments of high exaltation, you know that in a little while you shall see your ideal objectively as you walk through time and space. As within, so without. As above, so below. As in heaven so on earth. In other words you will see your beliefs expressed. Man *is* belief expressed!

BONUS BOOK

Believe in Yourself

Contents

1

Make Your Dreams Come True

J*oseph*, in the Bible, means "disciplined or controlled imagination." It is one of the primal faculties of mind, and has the power to project and clothe your ideas, giving them visibility on the screen of space.

Israel loved Joseph. *Israel* is the spiritually awakened man who knows the power of controlled imagination. It is called the "son of his old age." Son means "expression." *Old age* implies wisdom and knowledge of the laws of mind. When you become familiar with the power of imagination, you will call it "the son of your old age." Age is not the flight of years; it is really the dawn of wisdom and Divine knowledge in you. *Imagination* is the mighty instrument used by great scientists, artists, physicists, inventors, architects, and mystics. When the world said, "It is impossible; it can't be done," the man with imagination said, "It *is* done!" Through your imagination, you can also penetrate the depths of reality and reveal the secrets of nature.

A great industrialist told me one time how he started in a small store. He said that he used to dream (Joseph was a dreamer) of a large corporation with branches all over the country. He added that regularly and systematically he pictured in his mind the giant building, offices, factories, and stores, knowing that through the alchemy of the mind, he could weave the fabric out of which his dreams would be clothed.

He prospered, and began to attract to himself—by the universal law of attraction—the ideas, personnel, friends, money, and everything needed for the unfoldment of his ideal. He truly exercised and cultivated his imagination, and lived with these mental patterns in his mind until imagination clothed them in form.

I particularly liked one comment that he made as follows: "It is just as easy to imagine yourself successful as it is to imagine failure, and far more interesting."

Joseph is a dreamer, and a dreamer of dreams. This means he has visions, images, and ideals in his mind, and knows that there is a Creative Power that responds to his mental pictures. The mental images we hold are developed in feeling. It is wisely said that all our senses are modifications of the one-sense-feeling. Thomas Troward, a teacher of mental science, said, "Feeling is the law, and the law is the feeling." Feeling is the fountainhead of power. We must charge our mental pictures with feeling in order to get results.

We are told, "Joseph dreamed a dream, and told it to his brethren, and they hated him." Perhaps as you read this, you have a dream, an ideal, a plan, or purpose that you would like to accomplish. *To hate* is to reject in Bible language. The thoughts, feelings, beliefs, and opinions in your mind are the brethren that challenge you, belittle your dreams, and say to you, "You can't; it is impossible. Forget it!"

Perhaps other thoughts come into your mind that scoff at your plan or ambition. You discover that there is a quarrel in your mind with your own brethren; opposition sets in. The way to handle the opposition in your mind is to detach your attention from sense evidence and the appearance of things, and begin to think clearly and with interest about your goal or objective. When your mind is engaged on your goal or objective, you are using the creative law of mind, and it will come to pass.

"Lo, my sheaf arose, and also stood upright; and, behold, your sheaves stood round about, and made obeisance to my sheaf." Lift your ideal or desire up in consciousness. Exalt it. Commit yourself wholeheartedly to it. Praise it; give your attention, love, and devotion to your ideal; and as you continue to do so, all the fearful thoughts will make obeisance to your exalted state of mind—that is, they will lose their power and disappear from the mind.

Through your faculty to imagine the end result, you have control over any circumstance or condition. If you wish to bring about the realization of any wish, desire, or idea, form a mental picture of fulfillment in your mind; constantly imagine the reality of your desire. In this way, you will actually compel it into being. What you imagine as true already exists in the next dimension of mind, and if you remain faithful to your ideal, it will one day objectify itself. The master architect within you will project on the screen of visibility what you impress on your mind.

Joseph (imagination) wears a coat of many colors. A *coat* in the Bible is a psychological covering. Your psychological garments are the mental attitudes, moods, and feelings you entertain. *The coat of many colors* represents the many facets of the diamond, or your capacity to clothe any idea in form. You can imagine your friend who is poor living in the lap of luxury. You can see his face light up with joy, see his expression change, and a broad smile cross his lips. You can hear him tell you what you want to hear. You can see him exactly as you wish to see him—that is, he is radiant, happy, prosperous, and successful. Your imagination is the coat of many colors; it can clothe and objectify any idea or desire. You can imagine abundance where lack is, peace where discord is, and health where sickness is.

"His brethren said to him, 'Shalt thou indeed reign over us?'" Imagination is the first faculty, and takes precedence over all the other powers or elements of consciousness. You have 12 faculties or brethren, but your imagination, when disciplined, enables you to collapse time and space and rise above all limitations. When you keep your imagination busy with noble, Godlike concepts and ideas, you will find that it is the most effective of all faculties in your ongoing spiritual quest.

The phrase "Joseph is sold into Egypt" means that your concept or desire must be subjectified (Egypt) first before it becomes objectified. Every concept must go "down into Egypt," meaning into the subjective where the birth of ideas takes place.

"Out of Egypt have I called my son": Joseph is the commander of Egypt, which tells you that imagination controls the whole conceptive realm. Whatever prison you may be in, whether it is the prison of fear, sickness, lack, or limitation of any kind, remember that Joseph is the commander in prison and can deliver you. You can imagine your freedom, and continue to do so until it is subjectified; then, after gestation in the darkness, the manifestation comes—your prayer is answered.

Consider for a moment a distinguished, talented architect; he can build a beautiful, modern, 20th-century city in his mind, complete with super highways, swimming pools, aquariums, parks, and so on. He can construct in his mind the most beautiful palace the eye has ever seen. He can see the building in its entirety completely erected before he ever gives his plan to the builders. Where was the building? It was in his imagination.

With *your* imagination, you can actually hear the invisible voice of your mother even though she lives 10,000 miles from here. You can also see her clearly, and as vividly as if she were present; this is the wonderful power you possess. You can develop and cultivate this power and become successful and prosperous.

Haven't you heard the sales manager say, "I have to let John go, because his attitude is wrong"?

The business world knows the importance of "right attitude."

I remember many years ago having printed a small article on reincarnation. These pamphlets were on display on a book counter of a church where I lectured. In the beginning, very few of them were sold because the salesgirl was violently opposed to its contents.

I explained the biblical meaning of reincarnation to her, the origin of the story, and what it was all about. She understood the contents of the drama, and became enthusiastic about the booklets; they were all sold before my lecture series was completed. This was an instance of the importance of the right mental attitude.

Your *mental attitude* means your mental reaction to people, circumstances, conditions, and objects in space. What is your relationship with your co-workers? Are you friendly with people, with animals, and with the universe in general? Do you think that the universe is hostile, and that the world owes you a living? In short, what is your attitude?

The emotional reaction of the above-mentioned girl was one of deep-seated prejudice. That was the *wrong attitude* in selling books; she was biased against the book and the writer.

You can develop the right mental attitude when you realize that nothing external can upset you or hurt you without your mental consent. You are the only thinker in your world; consequently, nothing can move you to anger, grief, or sorrow without your mental consent. The suggestions that come to you from the outside have no power whatsoever, except that you permit them to move you in thought negatively. Realize that you are master of your thought-world. Emotions follow thought; hence, you are supreme in your own orbit. Do you permit others to influence you? Do you allow the headlines in the newspapers, the gossip, or the criticism of others to upset you or bring about mental depression? If you do, you must admit that you are the cause of your own mood; you created your emotional reaction. Your attitude is wrong.

Do you imagine evil of others? If you do, notice the emotion generated in your deeper self; it is negative and destructive to your health and prosperity. Circumstances can affect you only as you permit them. You can voluntarily and definitely change your attitude toward life and all things. You can become master of your fate and captain of your soul (subconscious mind). Through disciplined, directed, and controlled imagination, you can dominate and master your emotions and mental attitude in general.

If you imagine, for example, that another person is mean, dishonest, and jealous, notice the emotion you evoke within yourself. Now reverse the situation. Begin to imagine the same person as honest, sincere, loving, and kind; notice the reaction it calls forth in you. Are you not, therefore, master of your attitudes?

In reality, the truth of the whole matter is that it is your real concept of God that determines your whole attitude toward life in general. Your dominant idea about God is your idea of life, for God is life. If you have the dominant idea or attitude that God is the Spiritual Power within you responsive to your thought, and that, therefore, since your habitual thinking is constructive and harmonious, this Power is guiding and prospering you in all ways, this dominant attitude will color everything. You will be looking at the world through the positive, affirmative attitude of mind. Your outlook will be positive, and you will have a joyous expectancy of the best.

Many people have a gloomy, despondent outlook on life. They are sour, cynical, and cantankerous; this is due to the dominant mental attitude that directs their reaction to everything.

A young boy of 16 years going to high school said to me, "I am getting very poor grades. My memory is failing. I do not know what's the matter." The only thing wrong was his attitude. He adopted a new mental attitude by realizing how important his studies were in gaining entrance to college in order to become a lawyer. He began to pray scientifically, which is one of the quickest ways to change the mentality.

In scientific prayer, we deal with a principle that responds to thought. This young man realized that there was a Spiritual Power within him, and that It was the only Cause and Power. Furthermore, he began to claim that his memory was perfect, and that Infinite Intelligence constantly revealed to him everything he needed to know at all times, everywhere. He began to radiate love and goodwill to the teachers and fellow students. This young man is now enjoying a greater freedom than he has known for several years. He constantly imagines the teachers and his mother congratulating him on all "A's." It is imagining the desired results that has caused this change of attitude toward his studies.

We have said previously that all our mental attitudes are conditioned by imagination. If you imagine that it is going to be a black day today, that business is going to be very poor, that it is raining, that no customers will come into your store, that they have no money, and so on, you will experience the result of your negative imagery.

One time a man was walking the streets of London, and he imagined that he saw a snake on the street. Fear caused him to become semi-paralyzed. What he saw *looked* like a snake, but he had the same mental and emotional reaction as if it were a snake.

Imagine whatsoever things are lovely, noble, and of good report, and your entire emotional attitude toward life will change. What do you imagine about life? Is it going to be a happy life for you? Or is it one long series of frustrations? "Choose ye whom ye will serve."

You mold, fashion, and shape your outer world of experience according to the mental images you habitually dwell on. Imagine conditions and circumstances in life that dignify, elevate, please, and satisfy. If you imagine that life is cold, cruel, hard, bitter; and that struggle and pain are inevitable, you are making life miserable for yourself.

Imagine yourself on the golf course. You are free, relaxed, and full of enthusiasm and energy. Your joy is in overcoming all the difficulties presented by the golf course. The thrill is in surmounting all the obstacles.

Now let us take this scene: Imagine yourself going into a funeral parlor. Notice the different emotional responses brought forward as you picture yourself in each of the above-mentioned situations. In the funeral chapel, you can rejoice in the person's new birthday. You can imagine the loved one surrounded by his or her friends in the midst of indescribable beauty and love. You can imagine God's river of peace flooding the minds and hearts of all present. You can actually ascend the heavens of your own mind wherever you are; this is the power of your imagination.

"And he dreamed yet another dream, and told it his brethren, and said, 'Behold, I have dreamed a dream more; and behold, the sun and the moon and the eleven stars made obeisance to me.'"

In ancient symbology, the sun and the moon represent the conscious and subconscious mind. The 11 stars represent the 11 powers in addition to imagination. Here again, the inspired writers are telling you that disciplined imagination takes precedence over all other faculties of the mind, and controls the direction of the conscious and subconscious mind. Imagination is first and foremost; it can be scientifically directed.

I was examining one of the Round Towers of Ireland with my father over 50 years ago. He said nothing for one hour, but remained passive and receptive, seeming to be in a pensive mood. I asked him what he was meditating on. This is the essence of his answer: He pointed out that it is only by dwelling on the great, wonderful ideas of the world that we grow and expand. He contemplated the age of the stones in the tower, then his imagination took him back to the quarries where stones were first formed. His imagination unclothed the stones. He saw with the interior eye the structure, the geological formation, and the composition of the stone, and reduced it to the formless state; finally, he imagined the oneness of the stones with all stones and with all life. He realized in his Divine imagery that it was possible to reconstruct the history of the Irish race from looking at the Round Tower!

Through the imaginative faculty, this teacher was able to see the invisible men living in the Tower and to hear their voices. The whole place became alive to him in his imagination. Through this power, he was able to go back in time when there was no Round Tower there. In his mind, he began to weave a drama of the place from which stones originated, who brought them, the purpose of the structure, and the history connected with it. As he said to me, "I am able to almost feel the touch and hear the sound of steps that vanished thousands of years ago."

The subjective mind permeates all things; it is in all things, and is the substance from which they are made. The treasure house of eternity is in the very stones comprising a building. There is nothing inanimate; all is life in its varied manifestations. (The sun and the moon make obeisance to Joseph—imagination.) Truly through your faculty of imagination, you can imagine that the invisible secrets of nature are revealed to you; you will find that you can plumb the very depths of consciousness.

The other night I sat in a park and looked at the setting sun. Suddenly I began to think that the sun is like a house in the city of Los Angeles; there is a greater sun behind our sun, and so on to infinity. It staggers the imagination to ponder and meditate on the myriads of suns and solar galaxies extending into infinity beyond the milky way. This world is only a grain of sand in the infinite seashore. Instead of seeing the parts, let us look at the wholeness, the unity of all things. We are, as the poet said, "all parts of one stupendous whole, whose body nature is, and God the soul."

It is really out of the imaginative mind of man that all religions are born. Is it not out of the realm of imagination that television, radio, radar, super jets, and all other modern inventions came? Your imagination is the treasure house of infinity, which releases to you all the precious jewels of music, art, poetry, and inventions. You can look at some ancient ruin, an old temple, or pyramid, and reconstruct the records of the dead past. In the ruins of an old church yard, you can also see a modern city resurrected in all its beauty and glory. You may be in a prison of want or lack, or behind stone bars, but in your imagination you can find an undreamed-of measure of freedom.

Remember how Chico, the Parisian sewer cleaner, imagined and lived in a paradisaical state of mind called the seventh heaven even though he never saw the light of day?

Bunyan, in prison, wrote the great masterpiece *Pilgrim's Progress.* Milton, although blind, saw with the interior eye. His imagination made his brain a ball of fire, and he wrote *Paradise Lost.* In this way he brought some of God's paradise to all people everywhere.

Imagination was Milton's spiritual eye, which enabled him to go about God's business whereby he annihilated time, space, and matter, and brought forth the truths of the Invisible Presence and Power.

A genius is a man who is in rapport with his subconscious mind. He is able to tap this universal reservoir and receive answers to his problems; thus, he does not have to work by the sweat of his brow. In the genius type of mind, the imaginative faculty is developed to a very high degree. All great poets and writers are gifted with a highly developed and cultivated imaginative faculty.

I can now see Shakespeare listening to the old stories, fables, and myths of his day. I can also imagine him sitting down listing all these characters in the play in his mind . . . then clothing them one by one with hair, skin, muscle, and bone; animating them; and making them so much alive that we think we are reading about ourselves.

Use your imagination and go about your Father's business. *Your Father's business* is to let your wisdom, skill, knowledge, and ability come forth; and bless others as well as yourself. You are about your Father's business if you are operating a small store, and in your imagination you feel you are operating a larger store giving a greater measure of service to your fellow creatures.

If you are a writer of short stories, you can be about your Father's business. Create a story in your mind that teaches something about the golden rule, then pass that story and all its characters through your spiritualized and highly artistic mentality; your article will be fascinating and intensely interesting to your public.

The truth about man is always wonderful and beautiful. When writing a novel or story we should be sure that we clothe Truth in her garment of loveliness and beauty. You could now look at an acorn, and with your imaginative eye construct a magnificent forest full of rivers, rivulets, and streams. You could people the forest with all kinds of life; furthermore, you could hang a bow on every cloud. You could look at a desert and cause it to rejoice and blossom as a rose. "Instead of the thorn shall come up the fir tree, and instead of the briar shall come up the myrtle tree." Men gifted with intuition and imagination find water in the desert, and they create cities where formerly other men only saw a desert and a wilderness.

An architect of a city sees the buildings and fountains already in operation before he ever digs a well or builds a house. "I will make the wilderness a pool of water, and the dry land springs of water."

Long hours, hard labor, or burning the midnight oil will not produce a Milton, a Shakespeare, or a Beethoven. People accomplish great things through quiet moments, imagining that the invisible things from the foundation of time are clearly visible.

You can imagine the indescribable beauty of He Who Is being expressed on your canvas, and if you are a real artist in love with beauty, great beauty will come forth effortlessly. Moments of great inspiration will come to you; it will have nothing to do with perspiration or hard mental labor.

In Greenwich Village, I met a poet who wrote beautiful poems; he had them printed on cards, and sold them at Christmastime. Some of these poems were beautiful gems of spiritual love. He said that when he got still, the words would come into his mind accompanied by a lovely scene. Flowers, people, and friends would come clearly into his mind. These images spoke to him. They told him their story. Oftentimes the entire poem, song, or lullaby would appear complete and ready in his mind without the slightest effort. His habit was to imagine that he was writing beautiful poems that would stir the hearts of men.

Shelley said that poetry was an expression of the imagination. When the poet meditates on love and wishes to write on love, the Invisible Intelligence and Wisdom within him stirs his mind; casts the spell of God's beauty over him; and awakens him to God's Eternal Love so that his words become clothed with wisdom, truth, and beauty.

The Great Musician is within. If it is your business to play music or compose music, be sure that you are about your Father's Business. Your Father's Business is first of all to recognize God as the Great Musician; then meditate, feel, pray, and know that the Inner Music sings or plays through you the Song of God's Love, and you will play like you have never played before.

Every invention of Edison's was first conceived in his imagination. The same was true of Tesla, another great inventor and scientist.

I think it was Oliver Wendell Holmes who said that we need three-story men who can idealize, imagine, and predict. I believe it was the capacity to imagine and dream that caused Ford to look forward to putting the world on wheels.

Your capacity to imagine causes you, and enables you, to remove all barriers of time and space. You can reconstruct the past or contemplate the future thought through your inner eye. No wonder it says in Genesis: "Israel loved Joseph [imagination] more than all his brethren." Imagination, when disciplined, spiritualized, controlled, and directed, becomes the most exalted and noblest attribute of man.

I was in a conversation some years ago with a young chemist who stated that his superiors for years had tried to manufacture a certain German dye and failed. He was given the assignment when he went with them. As he commented, he did not know that it could not be done, and synthesized the compound without any difficulty. They were amazed and wanted to know his secret. His answer was that he imagined he had the answer. Pressed further by his superiors, he said that he could clearly see the letters "Answer!" in blazing red color in his mind; then he created a vacuum underneath the letters, knowing that as he imagined the chemical formula underneath the letters, the subconscious would fill it in. The third night he had a dream in which the complete formula and the technique of making the compound was clearly presented.

"Joseph [imagination] is a dreamer, and a dreamer of dreams." "They conspired against him to slay him. And they said one to another, 'Behold, this dreamer cometh.'" Perhaps as you read these Biblical quotations there are thoughts of fear, doubt, and anxiety conspiring in your own mind to slay or kill that desire, ideal, or dream of yours. You look at conditions or circumstances, and fear arises in your mind; yet there is the desire within you which, if realized, would bring you peace and solve your problem.

You must be like Joseph and become a practical dreamer. Decide to make your dreams come true. Withdraw, and take away your attention now from appearances of things and from sense evidence. Even though your senses deny what you pray for, affirm that it is true in your heart. Bring your mind back from its wandering after the false Gods of fear and doubt, to rest in the Omnipotence of the Spiritual Power within you. in the silence and quietude of your own mind, dwell on the fact that there is only One Power and One Presence. This Power and Presence is now responding to your thought as guidance, strength, peace, and nourishment for the soul. Give all your mental attention to recognizing the absolute sovereignty of the Spiritual Power, knowing that the God-Power has the answer and is now showing you the way. Trust It, believe in It, and walk the earth in the Light. Your prayer is already answered.

All of us read the story of Columbus and his discovery of America. It was imagination that led him to his discovery. His imagination plus faith in a Divine Power led him on and brought him to victory.

The sailors said to Columbus, "What shall we do when all hope is gone?" His reply was, "You shall say at break of day, 'Sail on, sail on, and on.'" Here is the key to prayer: Be faithful to the end; full of faith every step of the way, and persisting to the end, knowing in your heart that the end is secure because you saw the end.

Copernicus through his vivid imagination revealed how the earth revolved on its axis, causing the old astronomical theories to be discarded.

I think it would be a wonderful idea if all of us from time to time recast our ideas, checked up on our beliefs and opinions, and asked ourselves honestly, "Why do I believe that? Where did that opinion come from?" Perhaps many ideas, theories, beliefs, and opinions that we hold are completely erroneous, and were accepted by us as true without any investigation whatever as to their truth or accuracy. Because our father and grandfather believed in a certain way is no reason why we should.

One woman said to me that a certain idea she had must be true because her grandmother believed it. That is absurd! The race mind believes in many things that aren't true. What came down from generation to generation is not necessarily valid, or the final word and authority.

The above-mentioned woman, who was honest, and well-meaning, had a mind that was very touchy on psychological truths. She took everything in the Bible literally. This mind worked by prejudice and superstition, and opposed everything that was not in accord with her established beliefs, opinions, and preconceived notions.

Our mind must be like a parachute. The latter opens up; if it does not, it isn't any good. Likewise, we must open our eyes and minds to new truths. We must hunger and thirst after new truth and new knowledge, enabling us to soar aloft above our problems on the wings of faith and understanding.

The famous biologists, physicists, astronomers, and mathematicians of our day are men gifted with a vivid, scientific imagination. For instance, Einstein's theory of relativity existed first in his imagination.

Archeologists and paleontologists studying the tombs of ancient Egypt through their imaginative perception reconstruct ancient scenes. The dead past becomes alive and audible once more. Looking at the ancient ruins and the hieroglyphics thereon, the scientist tells us of an age when there was no language. Communication was done by grunts, groans, and signs. The scientist's imagination enables him to clothe this ancient temple with roofs; and surround them with gardens, pools, and fountains. The fossil remains are clothed with eyes, sinews, and muscles, and they again walk and talk. The past becomes the living present, and we find in imagination that there is no time or space. Through your imaginative faculty, you can be a companion of the most inspired writers of all time.

I gave a lecture on the 21st chapter of Revelation sometime ago in the Wilshire Ebell Theater in Los Angeles to our Sunday audience. The previous night while I was meditating on the inner meaning of the following verses, I intuitively and actually felt the presence and the intimate companionship of the mystic seer who wrote the inspired verses.

"And I John saw the holy city, new Jerusalem, coming down from God out of heaven, prepared as a bride adorned for her husband. And I heard a great voice out of heaven saying, Behold, the tabernacle of God is with men, and he will dwell with them, and be their God." (REV. 21:2, 2)

Can't you now walk down the corridor of your own mind, and there see, inwardly perceive, feel, and sense God's river of peace flowing through your mind? You are now in the Holy City—your own mind—inhabited by such lovely people as bliss, joy, faith, harmony, love, and goodwill. Your mind is clothed with God's radiant beauty; and your mood is exalted, noble, and Godlike. You are married mentally and spiritually to God and to all things good. You have on your wedding garment, because you are in tune with the Infinite, and God's Eternal Verities constantly impregnate your mind. In your imagination, you sense and feel that you are the tabernacle of God, and that His Holy Spirit saturates and fills every part of your being. Your imagination now becomes seized with a Divine frenzy. You become God-intoxicated, having received the Divine antibody, the Presence of God in the chamber of your heart.

You can look at a rock, and out of that rock through Divine Imagination you can reveal the Madonna, and portray a vision of beauty and a joy forever. Never permit your imagination to be used negatively; never distort or twist it. You can imagine sickness, accident, and loss and become a mental wreck. To imagine sickness and lack is to destroy your peace of mind, health, and happiness.

On board ship one time, I heard a passenger exclaim when looking at the setting sun, "I am so happy; I hope this lasts forever!"

How often have you seen a glorious sunrise, and perhaps you said, "I hope this lasts forever"? Nothing in this transitory world lasts eternally; however, the Truths of God last forever. Darkness follows night, but morning will come again. Twilight will also come. You do not want things to stand still. You do not want to stand still either, for there are new worlds within and without to conquer. Change eternal is at the root of all life.

You do not want to remain in a rut. Problems are life's way of asking you for an answer. The greatest joy and satisfaction is in overcoming, in conquering. Life would become unbearable and unendurable if we did not experience change. We would be bored by the monotony of things. You meet with night and day, cold and heat, ebb and flow, summer and winter, hope and despair, and success and failure. You find yourself moving through opposites; through your power to imagine what you wish to feel is to reconcile the opposites and bring peace to the mind.

In the midst of sorrow, grief, or the loss of a loved one, your imagination and faith—the two wings of the bird—take you aloft into the very Bosom of God, your Father, where you find peace, solace, and Divine rest for your soul.

In your imagination, you look into the very Face or Truth of God; and God wipes away all tears, and there shall be no more crying. All the mist and fog of the human mind dissolves in the sunshine of God's Love.

"And God shall wipe away all tears from their eyes; and there shall be no more death, neither sorrow, nor crying; neither, shall there be any more pain: for the former things are passed away. Behold I make all things new." (REV. 4:5.)

When the night is black, you see no way out; that is, when your problem is most acute, let your imagination be your savior.

"I will lift up mine eyes [imagination] unto the hills, from whence cometh my help." (Ps. 121:1.) The hills are of an inner range—the Presence of God in you. When you seek guidance and inspiration, fix your eyes on the stars of God's Truth, such as "Infinite Intelligence leads and guides me," or "Divine Wisdom floods my mind, and I am inspired from on High."

There is a designer, an architect, and a weaver within you; it takes the fabric of your mind, your thoughts, feelings, and beliefs; and molds them into a pattern of life that brings you peace or discord, health or sickness. You can imagine a life that will take you up to the third heaven, where you will see unspeakable and unutterable things of God; or through the distorted, morbid use of your imagination, you can sink to the depths of degradation.

Man is the tabernacle of God, and no matter how low a man has sunk, the Healing Presence is there waiting to minister to him. It is within us waiting for us to call upon It. You can use your imagination in all business transactions in a wonderful way. Always imagine yourself in the other fellow's place; this tells you what to do. Imagine that the other is expressing all that you long to see him express. See him as he ought to be, not as he appears to be. Perhaps he is surly, sarcastic, bitter, or hostile; there may be many frustrated hopes and tragedies lurking in his mind. Imagine whatsoever things are lovely and of good report, and through your imagination you have covered him with the garment of God. God's world of ideals and God's infinite ideas are within him, waiting to be born and released. You can say if you wish, "God waits to be born in him." You can open the door, and kindle the fire of God's Love in that man's heart, and perhaps the spark you lit will burst into a Divine Fire.

The greatest and richest galleries of art in the world are the galleries of the mind devoted to God's Truths and Beauty. Leonardo Da Vinci, through his gift of imagination, meditated on Jesus and the Twelve Disciples, and what they meant. Lost in deep reverie, his imagination secreted the perfect pictures from the Infinite Reservoir within him, and due to his perfect focus, his inner eye glowed with an interior luminosity, so that he was inspired, and out of his Divine Imagery came the masterpiece *The Last Supper.*

You have visited a quiet lake or a mountaintop. Notice how the placid, cool, calm surface reflected the heavenly lights; so does the quiet mind of the spiritual man reflect God's interior Lights and Wisdom.

Picture your ideal in life; live with this ideal. Let the ideal captivate your imagination; let the ideal thrill you! You will move in the direction of the ideal that governs your mind. The ideals of life are like the dew of heaven that move over the arid areas of man's mind, refreshing and invigorating him.

The inspired writer's imagination was fired with Truth when he wrote: "There is a river the streams whereof shall make glad the city of God, the holy place of the tabernacles of the most High." (Ps. 46:4.)

By now you know that imagination is the river enabling *you* to flow back psychologically to God. The streams and rivulets are your ideas and feelings, plus the emanation of love and goodwill that goes forth from you to all men everywhere. Man looks out into the world; and he sees sickness, chaos, and man's inhumanity to man. The man with the disciplined imagination soars above all appearances, discord, and sense evidence, and sees the sublime principle of harmony operating through, in, and behind all things. He knows through his Divine imagery that there is an Everlasting Law of Righteousness behind all things, an Ever-Abiding Peace, a Boundless Love governing the entire Cosmos. These Truths surge through the heart, and are born of the eternal Truth that through the imagination pierces the outer veil, and rests in the Divine meaning of the way it is in God and Heaven.

Imagination was the workshop of God that inspired the writer of the following matchless, spiritual gems—which will go down through the corridor of time and live forever. For tender beauty and for Divine imagery, they are unsurpassed in dealing with the availability and Immanence of God's Presence:

"For he shall give his angels charge over thee, to keep thee in all thy ways." (PS. 91:11.)

"Whither shall I go from thy spirit? or whither shall I flee from thy presence?"

"If I ascend up into heaven, thou art there. If I make my bed in hell, behold, thou art there."

"If I take the wings of the morning, and dwell in the uttermost parts of the sea; even there shall thy hand lead me, and thy right hand shall hold me."

2

Using the Subconscious Mind in Business

Long before our Bible was published, ancient wisdom said, "As a man imagines and feels, so does he become." This ancient teaching is lost in the night of time; it is lost in antiquity.

The Bible states: "As a man thinketh in his heart, so is he."

Legend relates that many thousands of years ago the Chinese wise men gathered together under the leadership of a great sage to discuss the fact that vast legions of brutal invaders were pillaging and plundering the land. The question to be resolved was: "How shall we preserve the ancient wisdom from the destruction of the invaders?"

There were many suggestions: Some thought that the ancient scrolls and symbols should be buried in the Himalayan mountains. Others suggested that the wisdom be deposited in monasteries in Tibet. Still others pointed out that the sacred temples of India were the ideal places for the preservation of the wisdom of their God.

The chief sage was silent during the entire discussion; in fact, he went to sleep in the midst of their talk and snored loudly, much to their dismay! He awakened in a little while, and said, "Tao [God] gave me the answer, and it is this: 'We will order the great pictorial artists of China—men gifted with Divine imagination [which is the workshop of God]—and tell them what we wish to accomplish. We will initiate them into the mysteries of Truth. They will portray or depict in picture form, the great Truths which shall be preserved for all time, and for countless generations yet unborn. When they are finished with the dramatization of the great Truths, Powers, Qualities, and Attributes of God through a series of picture cards, we will tell the world about a new game that has been originated. Men throughout the world for all time will use them as a game of chance, not knowing that through this simple device, they are preserving the sacred teaching for all generations.'" This was the origin of our own deck of cards.

The ancient Chinese sage, according to the legend, added, "If all the sacred writings were destroyed, they could again be resurrected at any time through the symbolic teachings and inner meanings of the various designs on the playing cards."

Imagination clothes all ideas and gives them form. Through the Divine artistry of imagination, these artists clothed all these ideas with pictorial form. In the act of imagination, that which is hidden in your deeper self is made manifest. Through imagination, what exists in latency or is asleep within you is given form in thought. We contemplate that which hitherto had been unrevealed.

Let us take some simple examples: When you were going to be married, you had vivid, realistic pictures in your mind. With your power of imagination, you saw the minister, rabbi, or priest. You heard him pronounce the words, you saw the flowers and the church, and you heard the music. You imagined the ring on your finger, and you traveled through your imagination on your honeymoon to Niagara Falls or Europe. All this was performed by your imagination.

Likewise, before graduation, you had a beautiful, scenic drama taking place in your mind; you had clothed all your ideas about graduation in form. You imagined the professor or the president of the college giving you your diploma. You saw all the students dressed in gowns. You heard your mother or father or your girl- or boyfriend congratulate you. You felt the embrace and the kiss; it was all real, dramatic, exciting, and wonderful. Images appeared freely in your mind as if from nowhere, but you know and must admit that there was and is an Internal Creator with Power to mold all these forms that you saw in your mind; and endow them with life, motion, and voice. These images said to you, "For you only we live!"

A young man said to me in the army before he was discharged, "I see my mother clearly. I can now imagine her welcome. I see the old home. Father is smoking a pipe. My sister is feeding the dogs. I can see every mark and corner of that home. I can even hear their voices."

Where do all these vivid pictures come from? Keats said that there is an ancestral wisdom in man, and we can, if we wish, drink of that old wine of heaven.

The spirit or God in you is the real basis of imagination. Once in an examination in London, I did not know the answer to an important question. I got still and quiet, and said over and over again slowly, meditating in a relaxed way, "God reveals the answer!" In the meantime, I went on answering the other questions, which were easy.

We know that when you relax the conscious mind, the subjective wisdom rises to the fore. In a short while, the picture of the answer came clearly into my mind. It was there in words like a page of a book, with the entire answer written out as a graph in the mind. A Mightier Wisdom than that of my conscious mind or intellect spoke through me.

I had a very religious school boy about 14 years old come to me. Whenever he had a problem, he said to me that he would imagine

Jesus was talking to him, giving him the answer to his problem, and telling him what to do. His mother was very ill; this boy was highly imaginative. He read the story of Jesus healing the woman with the fever. My little friend related to me, "Last night I imagined Jesus saying to me, 'Go thy way; thy mother is made whole!'" He made that drama of the mind so real, vivid, and intense that due to his faith and belief, he convinced himself of the truth of what he heard subjectively.

His mother was completely healed, yet she was considered at that time hopeless and beyond medical help.

Being a student of the laws of mind, you know what happened. He galvanized himself into the feeling of being one with his image, and according to his faith or conviction was it done unto him. There is only One Mind and One Healing Presence. As the boy changed his conviction about his mother and felt her perfect health, the idea of perfect health was resurrected in her mind simultaneously. He did not know anything about spiritual healing or the power of imagination. He operated the law unconsciously, and believed in his own mind that Jesus was actually talking to him; then, according to his belief, was it done unto him.

To believe something is to accept it as true. This is why Paracelsus said in the 16th century, "Whether the object of your belief be true or false, you will get the same results." There is only one spiritual, healing Principle and one Process of healing called *faith*. "According to your faith is it done unto you." There are many processes, methods, and techniques of healing, and all of them get results—not because of the particular technique or method, but because of imagination and faith in the particular process. They are all tapping the One Source of healing, which is God. The Infinite Healing Presence permeates all things and is omnipresent.

The voodoo doctor with his incantations gets results. So does the kahuna of Hawaii with his ministrations, the various branches of New Thought and Christian Science, the Nancy School of Medicine, osteopathy, and so on. All these schools of thought are meeting levels of consciousness and are doing good.

Any method or process that alleviates human misery, pain, and distress is good. Many churches practice the laying on of hands; others make novenas and visit shrines; all are benefitted according to their mental acceptance or belief.

When you are willing to stand alone with God and cease completely giving power to external things; when you no longer give power to the phenomenalistic world, which means to make a world of effect a cause; and when all your allegiance is given to the Spiritual Power within you, realizing it as the only Presence and the only Cause, you will not need any props of any kind. The Living Intelligence that made your body will respond immediately to your faith and understanding; and you will have an instantaneous, spiritual healing. If you are not at that level of consciousness where you can grow a tooth through prayer, the obvious thing to do is to go see a dentist. Pray for him and for a perfect, Divine, oral adjustment. As long as you believe in external causes, you will seek external remedies.

To illustrate further the power of imagination, I will tell you about a close relative of mine who had tuberculosis. His lungs were badly diseased, so his son decided to heal his father. He came home to Perth, Western Australia, where his father lived, and said to him that he had met a monk who sold him a piece of the true cross, and that he gave him the equivalent of $500 for it. (This young man had picked up a splinter of wood off the sidewalk, went to a jeweler's, and had it set in a ring so that it looked real.) He told his father that many were healed just by touching the ring or the cross. He inflamed and fired his father's imagination to the point that the old gentleman snatched the ring from him, placed it over his chest, prayed silently, and went to sleep. In the morning, he was healed; all the clinic's tests were negative.

You know, of course, that it was not the splinter of wood from the sidewalk that healed him. It was his imagination aroused to an intense degree, plus the confident expectancy of a perfect healing. Imagination was joined to faith or subjective feeling, and the union of the two brought about the healing. The father never learned the trick that had been played upon him; if he had, he probably would have had a relapse. He remained completely cured, and passed away 15 years later at the age of 89.

I know a businessman here in Los Angeles who has reached the top in his field. He told me that for 30 years, the most important decisions he ever made were based on his imaginary conversations with Paul. I asked him to elaborate, and he remarked that few people in the business world realized the wonderful guidance and counsel they could receive by dramatizing in their imagination that they were receiving counsel from the writers or great seers of the Bible.

I will quote this successful executive as accurately as I can: "Many times my decisions might have prospered the company or plunged it into bankruptcy. I vacillated, wavered, and got high blood pressure and heart disease. One day the idea came to me: Why not ask Jesus or Paul? I loved the Epistles of Paul, so when an important decision was to be made, I would imagine Paul was saying to me: 'Your decision is perfect; it will bless your organization. Bless you, my son! Keep on God's path.' After imagining I saw Paul and heard him, a wave of peace and inner tranquility would seize me; I was at peace about all decisions."

This was this businessman's way of receiving Divine Guidance by using his imagination to convince himself that right action was his. There is only one Principle of Intelligence in this world; all that is really necessary is to say and believe, "God is guiding me now, and there is only right action in my life."

The mind, as Troward tells you, works like a syllogism. If your premise is correct, the conclusion or result will correspond. The subjective reasons deductively only, and its sequence or conclusion is always in harmony with the premise. Establish the right premise in your mind; you will be subjectively compelled to right action. Inner movement of the mind is action. The external movements and action is the automatic response of the body to the internal motion of the mind. Hearing a friend or associate congratulate you on your wonderful decision will induce the movement of right action in your life.

The man who used St. Paul to impregnate his mind with the belief of right action was using the One Eternal Principle of Intelligence. His technique of arriving at that place in his mind does not really matter.

Goethe used his imagination wisely when confronted with difficulties and predicaments. His biographers point out that he was accustomed to filling many hours quietly holding imaginary conversations. It is well known that his custom was to imagine one of his friends before him in a chair answering in the right way. In other words, if he were concerned about any problems, he imagined that his friend was giving him the right or appropriate answer, accompanied with the usual gestures and tonal qualities of the voice, making the entire imaginary scene as real and vivid as possible.

I was very well acquainted with a stockbroker in New York City who used to attend my classes at Steinway Hall there. His method of solving financial difficulties was very simple. He would have mental, imaginary conversations with a multimillionaire banker friend of his who used to congratulate him on his wise and sound judgment, and compliment him on his purchase of the right stocks. He used to dramatize this imaginary conversation until he had psychologically fixed it as a form of belief in his mind.

Mr. Nicols, Ouspensky's student, used to say, "Watch your inner talking, and let it agree with your aim."

This broker's inner talking or speech certainly agreed with his aim to make sound investments for himself and his clients. He told me that his main purpose in his business life was to make money for others, and to see them prosper financially by his wise counsel. It is quite obvious that he was using the laws of mind constructively.

Prayer is a habit. This broker regularly and at frequent intervals during the day returned to the mental image in his mind; he made it a deep, subjective pattern. That which is embodied subjectively is objectively expressed. It is the *sustained* mental picture that is developed in the dark house of the mind. Run your mental movie often. Get into the habit of flashing it on the screen of your mind frequently. After a while it will become a definite, habitual pattern. The inner movie that you have seen with your mind's eye shall be made manifest openly: "He calleth things that be not as though they were, and the unseen becomes seen."

Many people solve their dilemmas and problems by the play of their imagination, knowing that whatever they imagine and feel as true, will and must come to pass.

Sometime ago, a certain young woman was involved in a complicated lawsuit that had persisted for five years. There was one postponement after another, with no solution in sight. At my suggestion, she began to dramatize as vividly as possible her lawyer having an animated discussion with her regarding the outcome. She would ask him questions, and he would answer her appropriately; then she condensed the whole thing down to a simple phrase, as suggested years ago by the French School of Mental Therapeutics. She had him repeat it over and over again to her. The phrase she said was: "There has been a perfect, harmonious solution. The whole case is settled outside court."

She kept looking at the mental picture whenever she had a spare moment. While in a restaurant for a cup of coffee, she ran the mental movie with gestures, voice, and sound equipment.

She could imagine easily the sound of his voice, smile, and mannerisms. She ran the movie so often that it became a subjective pattern—a regular train track. It was written in her mind, or as the Bible says, it was "written in her heart and inscribed in her inward parts." Her conclusion was: "It is God in action," meaning all around harmony and peace. (*Harmony* is of God, and what you want in a legal case is a harmonious solution.)

In the science of imagination, you must first of all begin to discipline your imagination and not let it run riot. *Science* insists upon purity. If you wish a chemically pure product, you must remove all traces of other substances as well as extraneous material. You must, in other words, separate out and cast away all the dross.

In the science of imagination, you eliminate all the mental impurities, such as fear, worry, destructive inner talking, self-condemnation, and the mental union with other miscellaneous negatives. You must focus all your attention on your ideal, and refuse to be swerved from your purpose or aim in life. As you get mentally absorbed in the reality of your ideal, by loving and remaining faithful to it, you will see your desire take form in your world. In the book of Joshua it says, "Choose ye this day whom ye shall serve." Let your choice be, "I am going to imagine whatsoever things are lovely and of good report."

I know and have talked to many people who diabolically invert the use of their God-given faculty. The mother, for example, imagines that something bad has happened to her son, John, because he is late coming home. She imagines an accident, a hospital, Johnny in the operating room, and so on.

A businessman whose affairs are prospering, yet dwells on negativity, is another example of the destructive use of imagination. He comes home from the office, runs a motion picture in his mind of failure, sees the shelves empty, imagines himself going into bankruptcy, an empty bank balance, and the business closed down . . . yet all the time he is actually prospering. There is no truth whatsoever in that negative mental picture of his; it is a lie made out of whole cloth. In other words, the thing he fears does not exist save in his morbid imagination; the failure will never come to pass, except he keeps up that morbid picture charged with the emotion of fear. If he constantly indulges in this mental picture, he will, of course, bring failure to pass. He had the choice of failure or success, but he chose failure.

There are chronic worriers; they never seem to imagine anything good or lovely. They seem to know that something bad or destructive is always going to happen. They cannot tell you one reason why something good should and could happen; however, they are ready with all the reasons why something dire and evil should occur.

Why is this? The reason is simple: These people are habitually negative; that is, most of their thinking is of a negative, chaotic, destructive, morbid nature. As they continue to make a habit of these negative patterns of thought, they condition their subconscious mind negatively. Their imagination is governed by their dominant moods and feelings; this is why they imagine evil, even about their loved ones.

For example, if their son happens to be in the army, they imagine that he is going to catch cold, become an alcoholic, or become loose morally; or if he is in combat, they imagine he will be shot, and all manner of destructive images enter their minds. This is due to the hypnotic spell of habit, and their prayers are rendered null and void.

Make a choice now! Begin to think constructively and harmoniously. *To think* is to speak. Your thought is your word. Let your words be as a honeycomb, sweet to the ear, and pleasant to the bones. Let your words be "like apples of gold in pictures of silver." The future is the present grown up; it is your invisible word or thought made visible. Are your words sweet to the ear? What is your inner speech like at this moment? No one can hear you;

it is your own silent thought. Perhaps you are saying to yourself, "I can't; it is impossible." "I'm too old now." "What chance have I?" "Mary can, but I can't. I have no money. I can't afford this or that. I've tried; it's no use." You can see your words are not as a honeycomb; they are not sweet to your ear; they do not lift you up or inspire you.

Ouspensky was always stressing the importance of inner speech, inner conversation, or inner talking. It is really the way you feel inside, for the inside mirrors the outside. Is your inner speech pleasant to the bones? Does it exalt you, thrill you, and make you happy?

Bones are symbolic of support and symmetry. Let your inner talking sustain and strengthen you.

"But the word is very nigh unto thee, in thy mouth, and in thy heart, that thou mayest do it. See, I have set before thee this day life and good, and death and evil."

Decree now, and say it meaningly: "From this moment forward, I will admit to my mind for mental consumption only those ideas and thoughts that heal, bless, inspire, and strengthen me." Let your words from now on be as "apples of gold in pictures of silver." An apple is a delicious fruit. *Gold* means "power." *Pictures of silver* in the Bible means "your desires." The picture in your mind is the way you want things to be. It is the *picture* of your fulfilled desire. It could be a new position or health. Let your words, your inner silent thought, and feeling coincide and agree with the *picture of silver* or your desire. Desire and feeling joined together in a mental marriage will become the answered prayer.

Be sure you follow the imagination of the Bible, and let your words be sweet to the ear. What are you giving *your* ear to now? What are you listening to? What are you giving attention to? Whatever you give attention to will grow, magnify, and multiply in your experience.

"Faith cometh by hearing," Paul says. Listen to the great truths of God. Listen to the voice of God. What language does He speak in? It is not Gaelic, French, or Italian; but the universal language or mood of love, peace, joy, harmony, faith, confidence, and goodwill. Give your ear to these qualities and potencies of God. Mentally eat of these qualities; and as you continue to do so, you will be conditioned to those positive, enduring qualities, and the Law of Love will govern you.

You have heard this oft-repeated quotation: "Man is made in the image and likeness of God." This means that your mind is God's mind, as there is only One Mind. Your Spirit is God's Spirit, and you create in exactly the same way, and through the same law as God creates. Your individual world; that is, experiences, conditions, circumstances, environment, as well as your physical health, financial states, and social life, and so on, is made out of your own mental images and after your own likeness.

Like attracts like. Your world is a mirror reflecting back to you your inner world of thought, feeling, beliefs, and inner conversation. If you begin to imagine evil powers working against you, or that there is a jinx following you, or that other forces and people are working against you, there will be a response of your deeper mind to correspond with these negative pictures and fears in your mind; therefore, you will begin to say that everything is against you, or that the stars are opposed to you; or you will blame karma, your past lives, or some demon.

Truly the only sin is ignorance. Pain is not a punishment; it is the consequence of the misuse of your inner power. Come back to the one Truth, and realize that there is only One Spiritual Power, and It functions through the thoughts and images of your mind. The problems, vexations, and strife are due to the fact that man has actually wandered away after false Gods of fear and error. He must return to the center—the God-Presence within. Affirm now the sovereignty and authority of this Spiritual Power within you—the Principle of all life. Claim Divine guidance, strength, nourishment, and peace, and this Power will respond accordingly, I will now proceed to point out how you may definitely and positively convey an idea or mental image to your subconscious mind. The conscious mind of man is personal and selective. It chooses, selects, weighs, analyzes, dissects, and investigates. It is capable of inductive and deductive reasoning. The subjective or subconscious mind is subject to the conscious mind. It might be called a servant of the conscious mind. The subconscious obeys the order of the conscious mind. Your conscious thought has power. The power you are acquainted with is thought. In the back of your thought is Mind, Spirit, or God. Focused, directed thoughts reach the subjective levels; they must be of a certain degree of intensity. Intensity is acquired by concentration.

To *concentrate* is to come back to the center and contemplate the Infinite Power within you that lies stretched in smiling repose. To concentrate properly, you still the wheels of your mind and enter into a quiet, relaxed mental state. When you concentrate, you gather your thoughts together; and you focus all your attention on your ideal, aim, or objective. You are now at a focal or central point, where you are giving all your attention and devotion to your mental image. The procedure of focused attention is somewhat similar to that of a magnifying glass, and the focus it makes of the rays of the sun. You can see the difference in the effect of scattered vibrations of the sun's heat, and the vibrations that emanate from a central point. You can direct the rays of the magnifying glass so that it will burn up a particular object upon which it is directed. Focused, steadied attention of your mental images gains a similar intensity; and a deep, lasting impression is made on the sensitive plate of the subconscious mind.

You may have to repeat this drama of the mind many times before an impression is made, but the secret of impregnating the deeper mind is continuous or sustained imagination. When fear or worry comes to you during the day, you can always immediately gaze upon that lovely picture in your mind, realizing and knowing that you have operated a definite psychological law that is now working for you in the dark house of your mind. As you do so, you are truly watering the seed and fertilizing it, thereby accelerating its growth.

The conscious mind of man is the motor; the subconscious is the engine. You must start the motor, and the engine will do the work. The conscious mind is the dynamo that awakens the power of the subconscious.

The first step in conveying your clarified desire, idea, or image to the deeper mind is to relax, immobilize the attention, and get still and quiet. This quiet, relaxed, peaceful attitude of mind prevents extraneous matter and false ideas from interfering with your mental absorption of your ideal; furthermore, in the quiet, passive, receptive attitude of mind, effort is reduced to a minimum.

In the second step, you begin to imagine the reality of that which you desire. For example, you may wish to sell a home. In private consultation with real-estate brokers, I have told them of the way I sold my own home; they have applied it with remarkable results. I placed a sign in the garden in front of my home that read: "For sale by owner." The second day after placing the sign, I said to myself as I was going to sleep, "Supposing you sold the house, what would you do?"

I answered my own question, and I said, "I would take that sign down and throw it in the garage." In my imagination, I took hold of the sign, pulled it up from the ground, placed it on my shoulders, went to the garage, and threw it on the floor, saying jokingly to the sign, "I don't need you anymore!" I felt the inner satisfaction of it all, realizing that it was finished. The next day a man gave me a deposit of $1,000 and said, "Take your sign down; we will go into escrow now."

Immediately I pulled the sign up and took it into the garage. The outer action conformed to the inner. There is nothing new about this. "As within, so without," meaning according to the image impressed on the subconscious mind, so is it on the objective screen of your life.

This procedure or technique is older than our Bible. The outside mirrors the inside. External action follows internal action.

I was engaged by a very large organization to do some spiritual work for them. Through fraudulent means, others were trying to lay claim to their vast mining and other interests. They were harassing the company by legal trickery, and trying to get something for nothing. I told the lawyer to dramatize vividly in his imagination several times daily the president of the company that he represented congratulating him on the perfect, harmonious solution. As he sustained the mental picture through continuous mental application, the subjective wisdom gave him some new ideas—as he said, "Right out of the blue!" He followed these up, and the case was closed soon afterward.

If a person has a mortgage due at the bank and he does not have the money to cover it, and if he will faithfully apply this principle, the subconscious mind will provide him with the money. Never mind how, when, where, or through what source. The subjective mind has ways you know not of; its ways are past finding out. It is one of the instruments or tools that God gave man, so he could provide himself with all things necessary for his welfare. The man who hasn't the money to meet the mortgage can imagine himself depositing a check or currency required in the bank; that is, giving it to the cashier. The important point is to become intensely interested in the mental picture or imaginary act, making it real and natural. The more earnestly he engages his mind on the imaginary drama, the more effectually will the imaginary act be deposited in the bank of the subconscious mind. You can take a trip to the teller's window in your imagination, and make it so real and true that it will actually take place physically.

There is a young lady who comes to our Sunday-morning lectures regularly. She had to change buses three times; it took her one-and-a-half hours each Sunday to get there. In the sermon, I told how a young man prayed for a car and received one. She went home and experimented as follows: Here is her letter, in part, published with her permission:

"Dear Dr. Murphy:

This is how I received a cadillac [sic]; I wanted one to come to the lectures on Sunday and Tuesdays. In my imagination I went through the identical process I would go through if I were actually driving a car. I went to the show room, and the salesman took me for a ride in one. I also drove it several blocks. I claimed the Cadillac car as my own over and over again. I kept the mental picture of getting into the car, driving it, feeling the upholstery, etc., consistently for over two weeks. Last Sunday I drove to your meeting in a cadillac. My uncle in Inglewood passed away; left me his cadillac and his entire estate."

If you are thinking, *Well, I do not know of any way to get the money to pay off the mortgage*, don't worry about it. To worry means to strangle. Realize that there is a Power inherent within you that can provide you with everything you need when you call upon It. You can decree now with feeling and conviction: "My house is free from all debt, and wealth flows to me in avalanches of abundance." Do not question the manner in which the answer to your prayers will come. You will do the obvious things necessary, knowing that the subconscious intelligence is directing all your steps, for it knows everything necessary for the fulfillment of your dreams. You can also imagine a letter from them mortgage company informing you that you are paid up; rejoice in the image, and live with that imaginary letter in your mind until it becomes a conviction.

Become convinced now that there is a power within you that is capable of bringing what you imagine and feel as true into manifestation. Sitting idly by, daydreaming, and imagining the things you would like to possess, will not attract them to you. You must know and believe that you are operating a law of mind; become convinced of your God-given power to use your mind constructively to bring into manifestation the thing you desire.

Know what you want. The subconscious mind will carry out the idea, because you have a definite, clear-cut concept of what you wish to possess. Imagine clearly the fulfillment of your desire; then you are giving the subconscious something definite to act upon. The subconscious mind is the film upon which the picture is impressed. The subconscious develops the picture; and sends it back to you in a material, objectified form.

The camera is *you* consciously imagining the realization of your desire through focused attention. As you do so in a relaxed, happy mood, the picture is cast on the sensitive film of the subconscious mind. You also need a time exposure; it may be two or three minutes or longer depending on your temperament, feeling, and understanding. The important thing to remember is that it is not so much the time as the quality of your consciousness, degree of feeling, or faith. Generally speaking, the more focused and absorbed your attention is, and the longer the time, the more perfect will be the answer to your prayer. *Believe* that you have received, and ye shall receive. "Whatsoever ye shall ask in prayer, believing, ye shall receive." *To believe* is to accept something as true, or to live in the state of being it; as you sustain this mood, you shall experience the joy of the answered prayer!

3

How to Imagine Success

God is always successful in His undertakings. Man is equipped to succeed because God is within him. All the attributes, qualities, and potencies of God are within.

You were born to win, to conquer, and to overcome! The Intelligence, Wisdom, and Power of God are within you, waiting to be released, and enabling you to rise above all difficulties.

There are many men who quietly use the abstract term *success*, over and over many times a day until they reach a conviction that success *is* theirs. Remember that the *idea of success* contains all the essential elements of success. As a man repeats the word *success* to himself with faith and conviction, his subconscious mind will accept it as true of himself, and he will be under subjective compulsion to succeed.

We are compelled to express our subjective beliefs, impressions, and convictions. The ideal way to succeed is to know what you want to achieve. If you do not know your right place, or what you would like to do, you can ask for guidance on the question. The deeper mind will respond; as a result, you will find a push or tendency in a certain field of activity.

The deeper mind is responsive to your thought. The subconscious—sometimes called "subjective or deeper mind"—sets in operation its unconscious intelligence that attracts to the individual the conditions necessary for his success. Man should make it a special point to do the thing he loves to do. When you are happy in your endeavor, you are a success.

Accept the fact that you have an inner Creative Power. Let this be a positive conviction. This Infinite Power is responsive and reactive to your thought. To know, understand, and apply this principle causes doubt, fear, and worry to gradually disappear.

If a man dwells on the thought, for example, of failure, the thought of failure attracts failure. The subconscious takes the thought of failure as his request, and proceeds to make it manifest in his experience, because he indulges in the mental practice of conceiving failure. The subconscious mind is impersonal and nonselective.

A business friend of mine, a tailor by trade, has a favorite saying: "All I ever do is add. I never subtract." He means that *success* is a plus sign. *Add* to your growth, wealth, power, knowledge, faith, and wisdom.

Life is addition! Death is subtraction. You add to your life by imagining whatsoever things are true, lovely, noble, and Godlike. Imagine and feel yourself successful, and you must become successful. You are never a slave to circumstances, environment, or conditions. You are a master of conditions. You can become a victim of conditions by mentally acquiescing to things as they are. As you change your mind, you change conditions.

A movie actor told me once that he had very little education, but he had a dream as a boy of being a movie star. Out in the field mowing hay, or driving the cows home, or even when milking them, he said, "I would constantly imagine that I saw my name in big lights in a large theater. I kept this up for years until finally I ran away from home; got extra jobs in the motion picture field;

and the day came when I saw my name in great big lights, as I did when I was a boy!" Then he added, "I know the power of *sustained* imagination to bring success."

What does *success* imply to you? You want undoubtedly to be successful in your relationship with others. You wish to be outstanding in your chosen work or profession. You wish to possess a beautiful home, and all the money you need to live comfortably and happily. You want to be successful in your prayers, and in your contact with the Universal Power within you.

Imagine yourself doing the thing you long to do, and possessing the things you long to possess. Become imaginative; mentally participate in the reality of the successful state; enter into that state of consciousness frequently; make a habit of it; then you will find you will be guided to do everything necessary for the realization of your dream. Go to sleep feeling successful every night and perfectly satisfied. You will succeed eventually in implanting the idea of success in your subconscious mind.

I know a drugstore clerk who was a licensed pharmacist receiving $40 a week plus his commission on sales. "After 25 years," he told me, "I will get a pension and retire."

I said to him, "Why don't you own your own store? Get out of this place. Raise your sights! Have a dream for your children. Maybe your son wants to be a doctor or your daughter desires to be a musician."

His answer was that he had no money! He began to awaken to the fact that whatever he could conceive as true, he could give it conception.

The first step toward your goal is the *birth of the idea* in the mind, and the second step is the *manifestation of the idea*. He began to imagine that he was in his own store. He participated in the act mentally. He arranged the bottles, dispensed prescriptions, and imagined several clerks in the store waiting on customers. He visualized a big bank balance. Mentally he worked in that imaginary store. Like a good actor, he lived the role. (Act as though I am, and I will be.) This drugstore clerk put himself wholeheartedly into the act . . . living, moving, and acting in the assumption that his store was his.

The sequel was interesting. He was discharged from his position, went with a large chain store, became manager, and then district manager. He made enough money in four years to make a down payment on a drugstore of his own. He called it his "dream pharmacy." "It was," he said, "exactly the store he saw in his imagination." He became successful in his chosen field, and was happy doing what he loved to do.

The individual who habitually maintains a mental attitude of faith and expectancy of the best is bound to succeed and advance in life. The individual who is depressed, dejected, morbid, and despondent attracts failure all along the line. Fear is truly a lack of faith in Divine supply. It is faith misplaced. Fear is faith in the wrong thing. Fear is a belief in lack, or that man's good is being withheld from him.

"Son, thou are ever with me, and all that I hath is thine." All things you need are in the invisible. It could be said that all things needed are in the abstract. You must desire to be greater than you are, in order to advance in life. Desire comes first, followed by a recognition of the Power within you enabling you to manifest what you want. The subconscious mind is the medium through which all that you desire can be brought into objectivity. You are the one giving orders in the form of habitual thinking, feeling, opinions, and beliefs. The subconscious mind obeys the orders given by the conscious mind. If your conscious mind is opposed to all negative thoughts, they can make no impression upon your subconscious mind. You become immunized.

If, for example, you say, "I wish I were healthy, then I could be much more successful in my work;" begin *now* to realize that your body is your mind expressed. The subconscious mind is the builder of the body, and controls all its vital functions. Your conscious mind has the power to change any idea or group of thoughts held in the subconscious mind. You can impress the idea of health on your subconscious mind when you know that it can be done. A conviction and sincere belief is necessary. Affirmative statements establish a definite impression on the subconscious mind.

A wonderful way to impress the subconscious is through disciplined or scientific imagination. By illustration, if your knee is swollen and you are lame, imagine that you're doing the things you would do if you were in perfect health. You might say that I would go downtown on a bus, visit friends, ride horseback, go swimming, or hiking. First, in your imagination you go on these psychological journeys, making them as real and natural as possible. *Continue* to go on these psychological journeys! You know that self-motivation is yours. All movement is first of the mind or consciousness of man before any external movement can take place.

By example, the chair does not move of itself. You must impart motion to it. The same is true of your body. As you continue to do all the things you would do were you healed, this inner movement will cause the subconscious to build the body in accordance with the image back of it.

The following is a wonderful prayer for perfect health. A minister I knew in South Africa applied this prayer and healed himself. Several times a day he would affirm slowly and quietly, first making certain that he was completely relaxed mentally and physically: "The perfection of God is now being expressed through me. The idea of health is now filling my subconscious mind. The image that God has of me is a perfect image, and my subconscious mind re-creates my body in perfect accordance with the perfect image held in the mind of God." This is a simple, easy way of conveying the idea of perfect health to your subconscious mind.

You can develop confidence by knowing and realizing that nothing can prevent you from achieving success. Develop a certainty in your mind that this Inner Power can be called upon to overcome all obstacles. There must be an assurance and determination on your part that you can achieve and accomplish what you set out to do. This positive, affirmative attitude constitutes confidence.

You have heard the Biblical expression "According to your faith is it done unto you." Faith in God is the realization that there is only One Spiritual Power that is Omnipresent, Omniscient, Omnipotent, All Love, All Light, All Beauty, All Life, and An Ever-Present Help in time of trouble. Know that His Power responds to your thought.

About the Author

A native of Ireland who resettled in America, Joseph Murphy, Ph.D., D.D. (1898–1981) was a prolific and widely admired New Thought minister and writer, best known for his metaphysical classic, *The Power of Your Subconscious Mind*, an international bestseller since it first appeared on the self-help scene in 1963. A popular speaker, Murphy lectured on both American coasts and in Europe, Asia, and South Africa. His many books and pamphlets on the auto-suggestive and metaphysical faculties of the human mind have entered multiple editions—some of the most poignant of which appear in this volume. Murphy is considered one of the pioneering voices of affirmative-thinking philosophy.

Printed in the USA
CPSIA information can be obtained
at www.ICGtesting.com
LVHW011140080824
787694LV00002B/217